The Logos and the New Mysteries

the logos
and the new
mysteries

MASSIMO SCALIGERO
Translated by Eric L. Bisbocci

Lindisfarne Books | 2019

Lindisfarne Books
An imprint of Anthroposophic Press / SteinerBooks
402 Union Street #58, Hudson, NY 12534
www.steinerbooks.org

Cover image: Rudolf Steiner's ceiling mural
in the first Goetheanum cupola
Design: Jens Jensen

LIBRARY OF CONGRESS CONTROL NUMBER: 2019934261

ISBN: 978-1-58420-923-2 (paperback)
ISBN: 978-1-58420-924-9 (eBook)

Printed in the United States of America

CONTENTS

So that your Light would shine

onto the Earth each day,

the ritual of Sacred Love,

whose virtue now reveals for you

the passage toward the New Mysteries,

has been performed

within the Earth's secret temple.

THE RESPONSIBILITY OF ESOTERICISM

I t can be shown easily how we must not expect the mechanistic limit—at which human culture has come to a halt—to be overcome by culture itself or by science but, rather, by spiritual sciences. The difficulty for culture to be aware of its present decline can be traced to the unfulfilled function of these spiritual sciences.

Science has been arrested at the quantitative sphere, not as a result of its own procedures, but because the system of these procedures has been deprived of the necessary inner counterpart, which should have come as an intuitive content from those who assume the task of advisers according to the principles of perpetuity. These advisers have simply analyzed the modern world. They have not uncovered the spiritual background behind the analysis. They have not been able to uncover the spiritual background of precisely the esotericism requested of them.

In effect, scientists and technologists conscientiously carry out their work. With respect to their task, they are in order, realizing what is relevant to them in each and every field. The same cannot be said of spiritual communities, whose task is to connect the human being to principles that are edifying.

Actually, the function of spiritual communities is not to echo past knowledge, but to penetrate current knowledge, or the knowledge from which the very research of the values of perpetuity moves. Their task should be to develop the knowledge required by the spirit with respect to the *present* state of civilization—to identify what the spirit wants through the experience of quantity and which connection with the human being it needs now beyond the connection it had in the past, before the reign of quantity existed.

By justifiably recognizing the level of the fall within the reign of quantity, spiritual brotherhoods seek the reconnection outside such a domain. They seek it in what preexisted, as if the spirit's process in time were not timeless. They seek it with present-day knowledge, whose dialectical limit is not overcome for the fact that one turns to doctrines whose limit as such was unknown. And, nonetheless, this knowledge has the power to interpret the Tradition and its texts, according to a *current* capacity of abstraction and of conceptual correlation, which were unknown to the authors of such texts.

The "past" is restored by means of a present *inner connection* that should be noticed. Not to notice it means to deprive the current human condition of the connection demanded by our present-day inner process, in which alone the force can appear. Not to recognize the connection demanded by the current situation means to be prohibited from encountering the force where it really continues on the basis of its perpetuity. Such perpetuity is the true Tradition, from whose present realization its nominal supporters involuntarily escape—dialectical estericists, notwithstanding.

Those who equate perpetuity with the temporal past, which is opposite the ongoing present, seek the ancient connection by means of the modern mind, which cannot be overcome by dint of a simple intellectual, mystical and philological reference to the ancient connection, because the modern mind is the product of the loss of such a connection.

The indication of the ancient connection believes it moves above the level of consciousness that allows it to move. It builds a system of values at this (level) by means of which it refutes it. It believes that it possesses a level that is higher than that upon which it establishes the edification and that it fundamentally ignores. It thus renders self-knowledge impossible, outside the reflected or dialectical form, from which it is unable to distinguish itself.

Despite noble intent, the inner impulse, and the regular philological apparatus, such brotherhoods renounce being aware of the knowledge that they implement and by means of which they propose a knowledge that should transcend it. Therefore, they build upon the unconscious.

Pointing to a metaphysical connection outside the knowledge from which they move, they divert spiritual research from the world's point of encounter with its original force, namely from the only point where the resumption of the interrupted path is possible. Consequently, the mechanistic reign of quantity proceeds unrelentingly, by continuing to eliminate the personality, quality, value, and the real human, everywhere. For this reason, the spirit, which nevertheless has within it the power to overcome, must pursue other paths.

Escaping from the mentioned brotherhoods is the original element of consciousness, called upon to respond to the cognitive demand of the sensory realm. And when some of them propose to overcome the "materialistic" level based on an analysis of the scientific process, such overcoming should be feared more than materialism itself, because it ignores the spiritual engaged in the sensory processes with its most elevated force, which corresponds to the noetic moment of self-consciousness. This moment, in which the original element of consciousness is expressed, be it even in the lowest form, is the impulse that, rendered conscious, has, within it, the power to overcome the limit of quantity. It is precisely this original element that the aforementioned brotherhoods ignore when they want to point out solutions or spiritual integrations for science. The "I" surfacing within the cognitive process that they intend to transcend escapes them.

At such a level, the misunderstanding is to pit the universal, mystically evoked, against the individual element that emerges.

Modern Gnostics replace the subject excluded from the reign of quantity and from its logic with a spiritual one that is transcendent and effectively unreal.

Materialism is born from the separation of logical structures from the real operator, which is the human subject. Formal or reflected logic becomes the logic of matter when the investigator fails to glimpse the connection of logical thinking to the "I." Outer objectivity acquires a power beyond the consciousness of the "I," from which it actually moves. Today, overturning the relationship spirit–matter is, nevertheless, unknowingly perpetrated even by esotericists who fail to glimpse the spiritual where it is rising—in the initial movement of self-consciousness, there, where logical intuition descends from the Logos. In reality, formal logic is not removed from the Logos only by the enthusiasts of quantity, but above all by those who presume to overcome it, those who fail to glimpse the source of the logical determination, there, where the Logos makes inroads into consciousness through the pure individual element.

They tend to superimpose onto the process of quantity the metaphysical Universal that they fail to glimpse in the process of self-consciousness—intimate to the "I," certainly not the reflection of the "I." For them, the "I" is the contingent or reflected "I," which is to be eliminated as a source of individualism, for the sake of an elevated "I," above the human, namely the universal with which they tend to integrate the mathematics of the physical world, science and technology according to the echo of the human being's past connection to its principles.

When Traditional esotericists speak of an absolute that is one and all, infinite and eternal, non-manifest and yet supports the levels of manifestation, one cannot but be in agreement with them. Yet, at the same time, one cannot but notice that they are limited to representing this absolute to themselves, or to projecting it outside themselves. They resort to thoughts whose category of infinite and universal they fail to recognize. They are unable to do so, because those thoughts are devoid of life. They demand their own specific spiritual practice, a modern spiritual practice, which the Tradition does not contemplate.

Traditionalists do not realize the truth or the original force of those thoughts, since they are unaware of the pre-dialectical path. Instead, they refer to a content that lies beyond them, but only insofar as they think it and simultaneously negate it as thought. Therefore, they envisage the universal presupposition, reducing the only available universal to an undetermined concept, but affirmed with the exclusive authority of the determination, unaware of itself—affirmed, therefore, dogmatically. Ultimately, the dynamic of such an affirmation of thinking is feeling—the position of naïve mysticism.

2

Science, Naïve Realism

Actually, the thinking that conceived the mathematics of the physical world, via the early investigators of the sensory realm—Copernicus, Galileo, Newton, Kepler, and so on—bore an unforeseen impulse, which it could cognitively connect to the sensory realm, to the level of quantity, or minerality, because it bore a new capacity—independence from ancient revelation, regarding forces that edify life by means of minerality. Such an impulse had never, until then, operated in human "investigating" as the conscious power of experimentation. But the consciousness of culture has yet to prove that it has grasped its sense.

Thought, dedicated to an object's mathematical and essentially physical representation, effectively gathers only the mineral value of this object. It ignores the internal structure. It only lets itself be moved by the physical "appearing" of the object, without considering its immeasurable being. The immeasurable remains only in such a movement of thinking—unaware. Consciousness rests on the *measurable*.

By dedicating itself to the object's pure mathematical element, thought must limit its own movement to the formal determination. It must draw the power of observation and determination for the object from itself rather than from mathematical presuppositions. That is to say, it demands from itself a moment of intuition *independent* of the soul, instinctively led to feel the inner content. It is thinking that bears the impulse of a new relation with the world—a relation unknown to pre-Christian Egyptian investigators, as well as to the Arab investigators of the Christian era. For this reason, the investigation of the sensory world conformed to the suprasensory universal. The mystical soul was part of it.

In truth, the actual object of observation and determination, as a purely measurable object, calls for thinking's independence of movement from the soul, that is, from that subjective matrix in which the psychic element, the mental and the cerebral are normally mixed. An inner element thus emerges that is inevitably free of psychism and of cerebralism, unbound to subconscious processes, to manifest according to the exclusive demand of what is calculable—pure objectivity. It can be said that the more thinking realizes it's a-psychic nature and its non-mentality, the more it is called to the exact conceptual determination of the physical–mathematical object.

If there is an essential element of thinking, of which there can be no doubt, like an original movement of certainty, it is precisely this: It manifests in the conceptual physical–mathematical determination. Thinking moves according to its own pure inner nature, since the determination carries with it its rigorous correlation.

Thinking's pure correlation with itself is, in fact, what is realized by means of the mathematical–physical correlation, which is valid objectively, but as a one-dimensional correlation of reality—the assumption of abstract quantity. Such a correlation is not the reality of the object or of the physical phenomenon, but an initial synthesis of thought with the *datum* of sensory minerality, where thinking nevertheless operates according to its own intuitive nature, which is essentially unmeasurable, or not identifiable with quantity, but capable of moving authoritatively within measurement and of connecting measurement with measurement.

Without its independence from the measurable datum, thought could not continuously operate from calculation to calculation, as it does from intuition to intuition, by means of the physical–mathematical theme. Such independence, however, is what remains unknown to the modern scientist—the physical, mathematical correlation ignores the pure conceptual relation that renders it possible.

There is a sensory datum that cannot but be perceived, or experienced. However, its sense is not derived from perception itself but, rather, from thinking—not from determined thinking but from its moment of will or conceptual determination—namely, the will and determination that were unknown to the traditional mental (activity), just as it can be noticed in the very structure, ideographic or hieroglyphic, of traditional languages, consistent with a psychic–imaginative process, rather than a conceptual one.

In a metaphysical sense, pure intuition can be recognized as the concept's inner mathematics, since it is the immeasurable power of form, of which the mathematical concept is nothing but the inferior projection.

When a formula is followed, or a theorem proven, the truth of the formula or of the theorem is not the path that symbolically expresses its construct but, rather, the internal mathematics of thought found within it. The error begins with the fact that, within that finding, thought does not recognize itself. It falls short of the mathematical spirit, by failing to grasp its own determination.

In mathematical–physical knowledge, the intuitive possibility of thought is aroused, not as a speculative, philosophical or moral process, but as a direct activity of the spirit that assumes the world in physical–mathematical conceptual form, based on sensory perception. But the spirit does not glimpse its own activity. This is the beginning of the error. The intuitive element is called upon to give its most spiritual contribution from the correlation of the world's pure minerality—the concrete objectivity, absolutely abstract, since it is limited by calculability. Such absolute abstractness is the guarantee of the purity of thought or of the a-psychic nature of knowledge, but it begins to constitute the impediment to this, to the degree that the spirit within it fails to recognize its own activity.

The reality of the intuitive process can be recognized by its being the concrete content of the experience. The process of reality, which normally identifies with sensory phenomenology, in the perceptual immediacy, unfolds in the "subtle body" or the etheric, which is in continuous movement according to the mobility or the forms and colors of the surrounding world. It is not matter that moves, but the immaterial etheric world, the same etheric that is the immediate vehicle of the intuitive process within the human being—identical indeed to the physical phenomenon, but not physical. That it is not physical is the ulterior experience, of which investigators must become conscious, insofar as they can become conscious of what occurs within them while experiencing physical objectivity.

They intuit a process that they believe to be a process of reality, because they see it unfolding within the phenomenon, but, if they are attentive, they can find that such a process and its intuitive content coincide. If they did not coincide, these investigators would know nothing of what occurs. They would not perceive the so-called process of reality.

The simplest phenomena of nature—the river that flows, the rock that falls, the vapor that ascends—would be nothing for observers if, etherically, their consciousness did not identify with them by unifying sensory notes, by connecting moment to moment, point to point, of the physical process. In reality, thinking, as an intuitive pre-dialectical movement penetrates perception—the content of perception emerges as a process of reality, which investigators consequently see unfolding outside them. They can see it unfolding outside them, to the extent that it, in actuality, unfolds etherically within them, appearing simultaneously within the phenomenon.

The scene where the intuitive process of reality unfolds is the investigator's consciousness. And a grave impediment to the human being's journey (possibly the gravest of the present time) is the fact that spiritualists who appeal to perpetuity are unable to recognize, within the coincidence of the phenomenon's internal process with its intuitive moment, the point where the spirit resumes its activity in the world. The original element of modern human consciousness—namely, the original element where one can exclusively begin to grasp the suprasensory anew—escapes.

The typical feature of physical–mathematical thinking is the pure determination by way of the physical object or the mathematical object, a determination that renders thought independent of the psyche by arousing its inner intuitive force. The essentiality of this is such that it acts as the object's content of truth, by means of its physical manifesting or as a mathematical representation.

Physical–mathematical manifesting is the support or path for the intuitive content. It is so identical to it that normally the experiencer, strictly attentive to the object, believes to reside within it or to receive from it. Indeed, the identity exists, but within the consciousness of the experiencer, not outside it.

Unawareness of the identity alters the vision of reality, legitimizing duality. It strengthens the world's abstract objectivity opposite the human subject, deviating the research itself. Technology is born and it is real, but it is not followed by original intuitive thinking—a thinking no longer aroused. The intuition is replaced by knowledge, but it is the knowledge that binds to an object and places it in an alterity opposite the intuitive thinking from which its truth has arisen. In the presence of the knowledge that rises to a spiritual value, original thinking is extinguished as an authentic spiritual (reality). It continuously retraces the process mechanically, not intuitively. This process ceases to be the process of truth.

It operates as the automatism of the alterity, cutting the object off from the intuitive current from which it is born. The alterity becomes real in itself as a process of mechanicalness, which conditions the human subject.

❈

Nonetheless, the intuitive moment's identity with the object is the real germ of the process. It is more real than the knowledge itself, which is its product. The identity is the foundation, but the foundation, ignored. It should constitute the high point of the research, since it is the higher experience of consciousness. Meanwhile, it is normally not even imagined as an initial occurrence. It is utilized without being recognized as an original moment of the process. Its own cognitive *product*, knowledge, obscures it.

Scientific knowledge, estranged at the moment of the intuitive identity, opens up the possibility to act upon the object and upon the physical–mathematical procedure, not by means of the initial cognitive forces of the identity, that is, not by means of a direct inner action but, rather, by means of an outer act, physically mediated—the action of one thing over another, according to the development of the process of the phenomenal or mathematical alterity. It is similar to the inductive–deductive process of logic, which can unfold automatically, apart from the original moment of thinking, and apart from the reality to which it refers.

Technology is born from science as an objective process that loses contact with the experience's initial spirit, acquiring a reality of its own, independent of the investigating subject, while it has no other presumption. Technological thinking definitively becomes unaware of the intuitive moment as the subject's identity with the physical–mathematical process. The germinal nucleus, from which the experience moves, is lost precisely at the level of experience.

Thus, Galileo, observing the oscillating lantern of the Cathedral of Pisa, intuits the laws of the pendulum, and each time from then on, scholars learn the story of that intuitive moment, insofar as it manifests to them as knowledge. But this knowledge—fixed and having become a concept—in its abstractness no longer gives rise to the experience of the original intuitive moment, except when researchers reproduce it meditatively within themselves, by rekindling its pure life. It is a rare event, but it is an indicator of the inner path that the research required.

The human being is cut off from the process of science and of technology, which becomes automatic according to the logical development within the alterity. The relationship escapes the subject, becoming the dead possibility of one object acting upon another and of this still upon another, according to a concatenation that ceases to be controlled by the human beings that aroused it, since they renounced the initial movement. Actually, they ignored it. They believe that the concatenation is valid only in its objective alterity. They do not recognize in that alterity the mechanicalness that has the foundation outside it and that, therefore, demands the connection with it from the depths.

The process of the concatenation, adverse to the direction of the intuitive moment from which it is born projected in the objective alterity, essentially posits itself as the limit of thinking to thinking, removing from human beings the possibility of conceiving a direct action on objectivity by means of the original element. For this reason, they start believing that the possibility to make the concatenated series of mechanisms act is progress according to an indefinite development, while they remain the passive gatherers of technological results in every field, and while the illusion of conquests decisive for the human being emerges along the indefinite line of mechanical progressivity.

Mechanical progressivity occurs and is necessary, but it lacks coordination based on inner necessity. It derives the coordination not from the subject but, rather, from the ironclad petition of its own development at that level, which should be controlled by thinking capable of recognizing the alterity as mechanicalness and of using it according to essential human intentions. In reality, we do not possess the thinking that connects technology to the spirit, for we lack original thinking. We cannot see, in the machine, the symbol of thought's temporary self-limitation.

3

FAITH IN THE PHYSICAL FACT

The intuitive impulse that gave birth to science is still unknown, yet we must return to it if we want to find the interrupted path of the spirit, not just the resurgence of science but, above all, the path to the suprasensory demanded by the new times, the future direction of science.

Knowledge that unconsciously contrasts with the original element of the determination according to an automatism of its reflected logic and, consequently, of its abstract dialectics, has been able to emerge from thought, born according to the pure determination of the object.

The error is not comprised of a logical or technological construct, indeed normal at its level, but rather, of the cognitive assumption that has eluded the original aim, or the logic of the essence and, therefore, the subject's responsibility. Thought identifies the object, but it does not see itself. It loses the pure moment of the determination, the germ of the research, without which it would not have an objective content. This, in fact, can arise to the extent that the subject of the experience unconsciously opposes it. Unaware of its own original power, it begins to come to pass as the subject opposed to the phenomenon or the objective datum—objectivity being its characteristic feature, which ensues from the original determination. This remains, however, the unknown determination.

Those of us who fail to operate as a subject would be unable to find our own determination in objectivity. We would be unable to find outside of us our own intuitive movement as the content of experience. Even when, on the plane of abstract mechanicalness, we forget the original moment of thinking and operate upon an object that appears immediate and first (but actually, it is second with respect to the intuited forces of the first object, so that an object acts upon another, and this, in turn, upon others), we remain the fulcrum of the experience. Even falling into the mechanism, this experience can make sense only insofar as it continues to have its fulcrum within the human subject.

Actually, even technology is a world inside of us, a system of values that unfolds within our consciousness, but within an alienated consciousness, which ignores its own original production and, therefore, bears within itself and simultaneously ignores the ultimate sense of such a system of values.

Even here, we are each the subject of the experience, since the realm of technology and, therefore, of the mechanism, asserts itself thanks to a missing sentiment of truth, which arises in us as intuition. It is not the original intuition, which has the possibility of determination independent of the object, but the intuition that has refrained from recognizing itself and, therefore, sees the presupposition in outer datum, in the phenomenon, in the fact. It does not recognize it within itself. Thus, its movement toward the object becomes conformity, dependence, and mystical submissiveness to its reality. Faith rises, but in the lowest form—as *faith in the physical fact.*

In truth, we do not go out of ourselves to possess the phenomenon, nor does the phenomenon enter into our heads. There is no physical transposition of the object or of the fact, as there should be if the materialistic assertion responded to truth. In reality, an immaterial phenomenology unfolds, so that a material "appearing" can manifest and can be thought, truly mediated by our etheric bodies, in continuous movement according to the etheric value of things—forms, colors, movement, and so on—not according to their materiality. Thanks to the etheric relation, the object, the fact, rises within consciousness as perception, representation, concept. The concept coincides with the object, from which arises the conceptual relation as a weaving of knowledge. By means of concepts, the subject relates objects to objects and facts to facts.

However, thinkers who are barely awake believe that they operate by means of objects, facts, phenomena, isolated outside them, foreign to their interiority—an interiority that we still lack the sufficient forces of consciousness to perceive. They believe it has something to do with things, and not with concepts. They believe in a material relation between things and not in a relation intuited between etheric forces that manifest by means of things. They do not perceive their own etheric bodies at the center of the relation, as its real fabric.

Insofar as it is intuitive and pre-dialectical, the relation connects one object to another. Researchers use this, but know it only in the dialectical phase. To know it as an original synthesis is the undertaking that can lead empiricism to an inner consistency with itself, which it lacks. Investigators do not move from one thing to another, but from one thought to another. They can place objects in relation to one another, insofar as they pursue them as concepts. In each perception, the principle of the concept is present, because, first of all, the subject is present, thanks to an immediate vehicle—pre-dialectical thinking. No perception exists without the presence of the subject within it—therefore, without the germ of the concept.

This pre-dialectical thinking, as the immediate presence of the "I," is itself whole. Nevertheless, it has two forms of its emerging—namely, the pure intuitive moment and the moment of pure perceiving—two moments that bear the power of synthesis and that thus originate the process of knowing, despite (being) pre-conscious, or pre-dialectical. Yet, we must emphasize that it is not a matter of transcendent moments, outside perception and thought but, rather, inherent within them—though not conscious. Thinking needs an act of will and freedom to be the vehicle aware of its own force, which is the force of the "I."

When one speaks of the immediate presence of the "I" within pre-dialectical thinking, one does mean to identify the "I" with it, but only its "flowing" in one of the two moments or simultaneously in both, thanks to the purity of the vehicle at its disposal—the intuition that thinks, the intuition that perceives. It is, indeed, the initial vehicle toward discovering a domain lost by the "I" and that, insofar as it is lost, rises before the "I" as a form of its alienation, that is, as an objective reality, an outer world, non-"I."

Yet, the lost domain is restored not by turning, via weak and reflected thought, to the evocation of forces whose spiritual doctrines indicate the perennial function but, rather, by perceiving the level at which such forces have become bound, as well as the point in which they, today, surface as the forces of self-consciousness.

The presence of the "I" within thinking is the power we modern humans use, while ignoring its existence. Because of the millenary custom to draw the sense of ourselves from the psychic element, in conformity—in past epochs—to the spiritual element, we today have a scant awareness of the birth of the immanent "I." We fail to notice the background of mathematical–physical thinking, whose function is to isolate the pure activity of thinking from the psyche, so that the "I" can recognize itself in the correlation. This correlation, lacking conscious *animadversio* (observation), ignores its original moment and identifies with its own projection, excluding the "I" by means of the "I"-forces barely born.

Within dialectical thinking, just as within perceiving, the pre-dialectical *dynamis* is the true sense of the experience, continuously present within it. But precisely such a *dynamis* is the value investigators believe they see outside of themselves; they do not notice seeing it as form, as concept. Within thinking, the *dynamis,* immanent, continuously solicited, is the atrium of the suprasensory world, which investigators seek within the sensory. Whether they turn to essential matter, whether they turn to an assumed world of super-matter, they illusorily seek, within the object, or above it, something that actually lies in the correlation—namely, in the identity with the object, in the non-conscious identity.

The essential, the original and pure energy continuously flow and are continuously lost in the physical experience. Investigators today are called "modern," because they can no longer have the essence mystically, or through faith. We have progressed. The original has become immediate to our consciousness. But consciousness, still as an obtuse mystical consciousness, tends to identify, outside of itself, the essential, the real that it has within it. It believes that it must refer to them rather than realize them. Dialectically or mechanically, it imagines the essence of things or of phenomena to be outside it to *believe* in them. It does not notice that such imagining is possible, because it moves from the essence.

Having relinquished the awareness of the experience's original moment, it has removed from science the possibility of knowing the human value of practical conquests. It has produced something for us, as humans, which begins to shut us off from the source of our creativity, insofar as such creativity is rooted in what *precedes* the dialectical–rational form in which it is expressed. Creativity has been arrested at the initial stage of its "manifesting." It has been arrested at its lowest point, or at the point of giving quantitative form to being—(a quantitative form) from which it is unable to move beyond. Meanwhile, all the problems posed by the present-day human organization actually demand, from science, this "moving beyond," which is not to insist on the same course, but to discover its original element.

An unawareness of the original course, or of the creative moment of knowing, has dried up, within the investigator, the connection with the essential. Our "investigating" is empiricism only in form. In substance, it expires into the unconscious *mysticism of the sensory*. The spiritual activity that moved the original investigators of the sensory realm has become stuck in cerebralism, which cannot have essential things but as simple names. It cannot have moral movement. The naïve mysticism of the sensory can hardly be identified behind the over-abundant analytical apparatus of reflected thinking.

We think by placing one concept in relation to another, but this relationship does not occur after concepts, but prior to them. The relation is the original synthetic movement. An identical original power of thinking forms concepts and unites them, according to an internal logic of each process of reality, bearing within itself, however, the force of the very principle of reality. The movement of the pure relation, identical to that of the intuitive nucleus of the concept, is in itself an unlimited *power of life*, from which dialectical consciousness is essentially closed off.

It would be a mistake to see, within the idea of the pre-dialectical power of thought, a philosophical theme; one is, in fact, before pure inner "experimenting"—namely, before the initial suprasensory perception, or before what alone can be considered an esoteric experience capable of overcoming the limit at which science has been arrested.

The movement of the pure relation is the pre-dialectical moment in which consciousness emerges, a consciousness that, however, grasps itself not where it emerges, but where it becomes estranged. In reality, it becomes estranged, because it is arrested at the point of manifesting dialectically, by temporarily expressing itself according to the cerebral, neuropsychic, corporeal support.

The movement of the pure relation, inhering to the support, does not explicate its free *dynamis* as an original synthesis. It does not know its own essence, because it becomes conscious according to the support, and it thinks the essence outside of itself. It sees the reality of the world, exterior and extraneous, powerful in its alterity, as though it had its foundation within itself, and affirmed its appearing in the form of matter. With the inner relation lost, the power of synthesis is utilized by the logical relation, which moves according to the appearing of matter, or of quantity, by means of an exact inductive–deductive process, that reflectively uses the synthetic original power, but by opposing it.

By eluding the "I," the *dynamis* of the relation, as a moment of freedom, becomes automatism, instinctiveness, material vision, and aversion to the principle, to the Logos. Such aversion is congenial not only to the materialist, but also to the spiritualist who, by following the dead paths of the Tradition, fails to distinguish the principle of the human being's disenchantment from animal nature, within the concrete element of knowing, within the pure relation.

The matter of materialism and the Kantian *thing-in-itself* are the same dead thinking—i.e., divided thought, which sees reality outside it and assumes it as truth apart from itself—matter, essence, God, the physical world, the metaphysical world. Not only does such a reality not exist, but its value normally escapes depending on the level of human knowledge; and escaping is (the fact) that a level of realized knowledge ceases to be true with respect to the immediately higher level. Slipping away is (also the fact) that, at a given moment, the "existing" of such a reality coincides with its being; this being, however, emerges as a correlation of the subject that perceives it, feels it and thinks it. Neither are the "perceiving"

and thinking processes separate from the reality of the world. This reality exists, but we fail to notice that, within us, it arises as an idea and that ideas are part of reality. But we cannot reach its core as long as we ignore its own ideating foundation.

Our error, our pain, is this *being* that lies outside us, devoid of the correlation that allows it to be. It is camped outside of us like a reality to which we cannot but conform according to the knowledge that it imposes, since such knowledge arises from the unawareness of the correlation, that is, from thought that does not see the idea from which it moves. Thought does not grasp the correlation, because it does not manage to grasp itself. It does not manage to think itself. It is thought that establishes the world, but does not know how to establish itself. It is thought that produces materialism, because it excludes matter from itself. It fetishizes matter because it unknowingly idealizes it.

Idealism is not a negative reality when it is conscious of its ideal process. It becomes a misunderstood reality when it deems itself to be materialism. It does not know that it establishes its edifice on the *idea* of matter. Materialists are precisely the ones who prohibit themselves from knowing matter, because, unknowingly, they make a presupposition out of it, essentially valid only as thought, which for them, however, coincides with reality.

Thought that does not manage to penetrate itself does not penetrate matter. Powerless before matter, it *believes* in it as (if it were) a foundation that stands, objective, opposite it. In essence, the relation that thought establishes with matter is a relation of faith—an obscure residual of the ancient faith.

4

FORMS OF DRUGS:
MYSTICAL, CORPOREAL, AND DIALECTICAL

M atter not penetrated by thought arouses its mysticism in various forms, from the scientific to the religious. Unawareness of the inner content of perception leads to an inadequate experience of the world or to the world devoid of Logos. Indeed, this non-perception of the Logos generates the deification of matter, or materialism.

No different is the case that leads the current revivification of the tradition of mysticism, Theosophy, alchemy, hermeticism, and so on to that subtle form of materialism that is the idolatry of symbols, of names, of short prayers, and so on, because it seeks the Logos where it no longer is, in the tomb from which instead the Logos has risen, by being born as the inner life of the soul, as the pre-dialectical life of thought.

Gnosis becomes revivified, to the extent that one correctly perceives that the Logos can no longer be found within present-day dialectical consciousness. But one commits the error of seeking it in past forms, without escaping dialectical consciousness, because one does not have available what overcomes it. One does not discern where, within consciousness, the Logos is about to emerge. The revivification of *mysteriosophy,* although it utilizes the forms of the Tradition, does not escape dialectical conditioning. Rather, it undergoes it more thoroughly, because it believes itself to be outside it. By ignoring the inner technique needed to penetrate the modern phenomenon of dialectics, it ignores the passage from the dialectical to the pre-dialectical, or from the human–animal element to the original human.

Mysteriosophy, formally revivified, is unaware of being cut off from the living current of ancient gnosis. It itself is a dialectics, whose inner counterpart is provided by mediumship and mystical feeling, incapable of overcoming the subjective limit, which coincides precisely with the dialectical limit.

Mediumship and mystical feeling, incapable of being independent of the enchantment of matter, constitute the same level—the level *animically** inferior to that of the sciences of quantity, for it is devoid of the level of awareness demanded by the dialectics of the mathematical–physical determination. Therefore, there does not exist a materialism more obtuse than what, in the name of an abstract evolution of consciousness, tends, for example, to undermine the traditional element of the liturgy in the Church and to arrive at the desecration of the Mass, which instead should be left intact in the traditional form, precisely with respect to the evolutionary aims of present-day consciousness, which must succeed in resounding according to the original contents and not have these adapt to its decadent dialectics and correlative hysterias. The traditional form of the Mass is needed not only by the human type still immersed in the sentient soul, or even by seekers still capable of arriving (by means of it) at an evocation of the mysteries, but above all by adolescents and by young people prior to the age of being consciously responsible—especially by these. Children regularly mythicize according to truth. Bearing spontaneously the objective element of the fairytale, they have the rare power of lifting a sensory datum to the suprasensory level. Therefore, they can

---

* The words *animic* and *animically,* though rarely used in English, have been employed in this translation for the Italian word *animica* (or *animico*), which has its basis in the word *anima* (or soul). It corresponds in Anthroposophy to the astral body.

experience the content of the mysteries by way of immediate inner communion. To deprive them of these in the sacraments means to corrupt, in them, the vital lifeblood of the soul, by means of inverse myth-making.

Such misunderstandings are possible at the level of fallen thought and as presumptions of an agnostic revivification of the sacred, characterized by its "ignoring" of the current contradiction of thought within the life of the soul, radically opposed to the Logos. In fact, it instinctively opposes the science of the spirit, or the knowledge that provides an opportunity to penetrate (via the volitional element of consciousness) the process by means of which thought becomes the vehicle of liberation, precisely by moving initially from the opposition, that is, by becoming conscious of it and overcoming it. An overcoming of the human–animal element is not possible—which, among other things, is expressed in impulses of desecration—without an awareness of thought's dialectical opposition to the Logos.

It is precisely the doctrines that seem to indicate the paths of the Logos, of mysticism, of devotion, which undermine our chance to reawaken the sentiment of divine things, since they ignore the technique demanded by our changed inner constitution. Their occult function is to divert our modern-day quest for the Logos, no differently than materialism. A peculiar kind of materialism, in fact, is what believes itself to be spiritual, insofar as it uses the names of the spirit, with confidence, mystically philological. Philological mysticism is the sublimation of dialectical pedantry proper to reflected thinking, bound, in any case, to its own sterility, irrespective of the esoteric impulses.

Dialectical thought is so identical to its own reflected dimension that it is unable to conceive any other. Even when it believes that it conceives living thinking, it unknowingly reduces it to its own scale, by imagining it to be reflected in movement. This explains how from philosophizing, or from idealism, a liberating spiritual practice has been unable to emerge.

As a dimension of powerlessness, reflected thinking does not conceive a freedom that is not the manifesting of its own dimension in another form. Therefore, it comes to believe, among other things, in a spiritual experience outside the spirit, which can be attained by means of philological processes specifically provoked. It can believe in the efficacy of substances such as mescaline, lysergic acid, psilocybin, and so on, as vehicles to the suprasensory.

Regarding drugs, we can say that they constitute an illusory inner path, with respect to which the weak become annihilated. The strong are introduced to a demonic magic, or a magic pact, whereby the soul has succumbed to sub-material forces from which it will no longer free itself—unless by the miracle of a Faustian type of redemption, truly rare. Healthy individuals, who are truly strong, tragically struggle to free themselves of it.

The misunderstanding of drugs is linked to the obscure aspiration to overcome the prison of reflected consciousness. Such aspiration is unable to rise to an awareness of the task that corresponds to it, namely to comprehend the passage from reflected thought to living thinking, or from the organ of error—true only when it is the measure of the calculable—to the organ of truth, or of reality. Only living thinking can perceive the nonreality of reflected thought. With reflected thought, it is not possible to grasp the reality of living thinking, the absolute diversity, the transcendent dimension. Experience is needed, but this experience demands the spiritual practice of the will, which is precisely the path of thinking.

The path of drugs is easy, because it does not demand inner initiative, but only sensory mediation that gives reflected thought the illusion of overcoming the sensory limit. Only materialists can believe that they overcome material vision by means of a material vehicle. The unawareness of the cosmic forces operating at the heart of matter inexorably keeps each of us captive to matter.

Erroneously, it is believed that the physical process aroused by drugs or by physical disciplines—such as alterations of hatha yoga—can remove from sensory perception, the obstruction that conceals the suprasensory from us. This obstruction occurs within the sense organs by means of the nervous system, due to the fact that thinking becomes conscious and dialectical by binding itself to the cerebral organ.

The exclusively physical vision of reality arises from ties to the nervous system, since such a system is controlled by the cosmic entity that lives in physical matter—though not in matter as it appears to us but, rather, at a subsensory level, which is the darkness of matter, in a sphere that has its manifestations, its forces, its extrasensory processes. It is this entity that can control us by means of reflected thinking, since the level of reflected thought is that in which this entity is the ruler and can hide the suprasensory from us. It controls the support necessary to thinking to grasp itself in a reflected state.

From the reflected state, thinking can free itself only by means of the self-movement that takes advantage of the foundation, or of its pre-reflected or pre-cerebral being. Drugs, instead, strengthen thought's subjection to the reflected state; they exalt reflectivity, by way of the nervous system, until making of it the animation of the phantom, whose form corresponds to content, since this is not derived from the spiritual but, rather, from the animic (soul) overcome by the physical. It does not overcome the sensory. On the contrary, it undergoes it, pathologically, more than ever because it descends below the sensory level, or to a level lower than that of normal sensory perception.

The morbid state aroused because of the nervous system is translated into vision. The ahrimanic entity that controls the nervous system and grasps the soul the more this soul inheres to such a system acquires through drugs a radical power over the soul.

The ahrimanic entity manages to provide extrasensory vision, by means of possession, but it is a vision of the realm that this entity controls—the subsensory, or the infernal power of the sensory. It is the realm of forces normally valid by way of the nervous system. However, by ruling fundamentally from the bones, or from the skeleton, at the level of everyday consciousness, they deprive the inner human of suprasensory perception within the sense organs. They grant it the physical or exclusively mineral vision of the world—and this is their legitimate task—rendering thought reflected or dialectical. But it is the realm of death, Hades, the realm of the shadows.

Drugs can make the ahrimanic realm of the shadows sparkle, enlivening it with the overpowered current of the drugged soul. The visionary and laudatory poetics of that world comes from the luciferic entity, while the power of hallucination comes from Ahriman. It is a power that in certain subjects can temporarily take on form and magical presumption, to the extent that the soul has the impulse to completely abdicate its own principle and unscrupulously open up to ahrimanic obsession, thereby allowing itself to be possessed by it. It receives from it a force of detachment from emotions and from passions, which gives the sense of human control. It is instead the paralysis of feeling. Weak subjects do not arrive at this and they are pushed evermore, by anguish and everyday fear, toward intoxication and, therefore, prematurely led to the realms of the shadows.

Anguish and fear constitute the corrective residue of the soul's inner element. In essence, those who suffer and struggle, by going through tragic experiences, are the subjects for which there is hope that the soul can respond on behalf of its residual autonomy. Those who instead strengthen themselves through a kind of "magic pact" have something to share with Ahriman, the powerful ruler of the nervous system, where magical forces are hidden, which the disciple of the "solar path" is responsible for conquering by descending as a conscious ruler into those depths.

Those who take drugs and draw psychic energies from them are subjects that have directorial ahrimanic tasks at the center of occult brotherhoods, whose goal is the fight against the inner human being—in reality, against the Logos. They have the task of corrupting the multitude by spreading the myth that the extrasensory is attainable through physical means, drugs, or magical mediumship, or distorted hatha yoga—the future path of the loss of the human level.

The process of liberation truly centers on the question of reflected thought, since human choice is determined at the level of reflected thought. We are free to choose between the Logos and Ahriman. The real initiatory path is the one that leads spiritual practitioners to the awareness of reflected thought and of its limit. It leads them to acknowledge, by way of the suprasensory experience, the overcoming of reflectivity as an essential condition.

Identifying with reflectivity leads consciousness to conceive the absurdity of a suprasensory experience by means that are extraneous, or opposed, to the suprasensory. In tantra, what is limitlessly considered acceptable to the "left hand" path is a concept that has to do with reflected or fallen thinking. A distinction between the left hand and the right hand is meaningless to living thinking, because the thinking force needs neither permissible nor non-permissible mediations for a suprasensory experience. It has its own authority within itself. It does not depend on categories of thought, right or left.

The path of the thinking–Logos is the direct path, in relation to which each mediation that proves to be merely preliminary, or preparatory, must be in line with a rigorous discipline. The task of those who are yet to be ready or who do not feel themselves capable of the direct path—and they constitute the majority—is to conform to norms and to disciplines, whose regularity lies in being derived from whoever possesses the direct path, given, as a matter of fact, by the Master of the New Times [i.e., Rudolf Steiner]. The guarantee of the legitimacy of this is its presupposition, the spiritual practice of the will, the path of thinking, which appeals to the conscious thinking of normal waking life and leads it, through intensified concentration, to draw on its original force, until identifying itself with it and overcoming the reflected dimension.

In the era of absolute reflected or dialectical thought, in which the soul undergoes, as obtuseness, the level to which fallen thought confines it, each inner development that does not follow the ascending line of waking consciousness cannot but be mediumistic and, in that respect, it is minimally a drug. A mystical, or spiritualistic, or gnostic–mediumistic drug, according to a range that extends to the drug in the strict sense of the word, it is the inevitable choice of dialectical thought, incapable of grasping its own reflected dimension.

To grasp the real sense of reflectivity, thinking must perceive the dimension that is simultaneous to it on the suprasensory level—which is the secret of its reintegration. Thinking simultaneously lives in three worlds—physical, animic, and spiritual. By moving down, it simultaneously moves up. It must intensify the momentum of its own force to perceive itself wholly according to the principle of the proper concentration.

One form of the modern psychic drug is the myth of animal evolution. Reflected thought, devoid of the movement of self-knowledge, conceives a material evolution according to a concatenation of rings, the first of which, however, escapes it. It is the most important, which lies within it, surfacing in fact as the awareness of the evolutionary process, or intuitive moment of a being, which, as a being in its "becoming," cannot but essentially coincide with the original movement itself of the concatenation. At the same time, there is no connection from one ring to another that is not the synthetic path of thinking, which follows the thread of that initial movement. It would be unable to follow this thread if it did not have it within itself.

No moment of evolution exists that, for the investigator, is not the movement of thinking, which grasps that moment and connects it with the others. Without the capacity of the original connection of thinking, biological evolution would be inconceivable. However, it is conceivable when thought realizes the relation within itself, having completed its own path up to self-consciousness, so that it can summarize it. It summarizes it when the spiritual impulse from which it moves becomes the force of determination for the investigation of a physiological phenomenon. As conscious thought, it is the chain's ultimate ring, capable of agreeing with the process and of identifying it. It is this last ring that, if it is capable of perceiving itself, can recognize itself as the first, given that it flourishes directly from the principle of the concatenation.

Biological evolution is real. The error of its doctrine is that of not being completely logical, or of not recognizing, in the reconstitution of the concatenation of the biological forms, the decisive ring as an occurrence of thinking, which flows from the principle independent of the process, or rather, its ruler. Evolutionists who use the concatenation of thought and believe they recognize, within the concatenation of forms, an outer process (as if one form issued from another outside of the inner connective process independent of each and every form), risk not seeing the genuine principle that unites one form to another and that in each form expresses itself ever more precisely. They are at the risk of believing in an animal origin of the human being. But they cannot avoid falling into such a trap, when they *believe* in facts and not in the thinking that intuits them and interprets them, and when they do not recognize, as thought, the conductive thread of the evolution that they conceive.

For this reason, this thread cannot help them when they, seeking the initial ring, do not find it. They clutch the void and vent themselves in theories that betray the mystical viewpoint—believing in facts and demonstrations, while ignoring the thinking that intuits facts and produces demonstrations, possessing within itself the synthetic power that unites them.

If the first link of the evolutionary chain is missing, the whole succession falls apart, since there is no a chain without the first link. And if one considers the second as the first, or the ring immediately graspable, one risks considering the primary element as the derivative. This is to overturn the process as it really is and to be of the opinion that humans come from apes.

Modern analytical logic behaves no differently with deduction, which can be correct in its formal concatenation, while always lacking the first ring, which it substitutes with an initial enunciation, or presupposition, or axiom—namely, the illusory foundation, or the clay foundation of the logical edifice, of the foundation of each and every rationale of so-called reality.

Actually, the pure relation, prior to concepts, originally connects one thought to another, one concept to another, and one idea to another. For sensory research, the determination of thought begins by soliciting it, but at a later stage it loses it—the stage of phenomenology and of the logical procedure.

A given thought is not determinative thinking. It is reflected thought, which loses the original relation because it ignores assuming this relation, and it utilizes it by overlooking it. But, although it loses this relation, it preserves its function, altered. At the level of reflectivity, it utilizes the original relation between one thing and another. This relation cannot be between one thing and another, or between one point of matter and another, or between one measurement and another but, rather, between one concept and another. Between one thing and another, there truly cannot exist any relation but that of thought—indeed, the original one, which, reflected, however, cannot but be abstract or non-real, in its objectivity.

The mathematical relation is true, but it is not the relation of the essence. It takes place between groups of sensory notes or sets of particulars of an identical entity, but not as an organic relation of such an entity or of different entities—not as a substantial unity but, rather, as a partial relation of the multiplicity, to which other partial relations of the multiplicity of the same entity can be opposed. It is the particular knowledge that, by tending to be of value as a universal, distorts the unity of any organic process by connecting one detail to another, outside the original relation, according to the immediate quantitative relation, which moves in formal regularity, consistent with an abstract aspect, or separated from other aspects of the same content. From this, its functioning arises as an ideological drug. From such formal regularity a formative force escapes—the true content, as a unitary content.

It is not the true relation, but only its symbol—a symbol devoid of essence. It is a relation that is mechanical, exact, but devoid of reality. That void is inhabited by error, because present within it is not the inner reality of the object but, rather, instinct, the inferior faith of the "quantumly" measured—namely the a-critical faith in modernly legitimate, logical–mathematical guise. The logical–materialistic economy, for example, no longer grasps the economic process, which once, instead, was controlled by human beings endowed with concrete intuition, even if (they were) oblivious to economic sciences.

From the mental realm devoid of an original synthetic movement, there arises the naïve idea that social justice is attainable through a legal mathematical (if not constrictive) distribution of goods, rather than a free inner process—free and, therefore, moral. It is inconceivable that the distributive mathematics of goods will ever achieve anything—instead, it will worsen the situation that already exists—if, at its core, it does not have inner values such as the autonomy of the individual initiative, the recognition of specific spiritual vocations in every field, the awareness of the absolutely extrapolitical value of the spiritual principle.

There, where thinking dies to its own current of life, it becomes dialectical and conscious. But there, for example, where this thinking presumes to direct an economic process, it inevitably eliminates, within this process, the cohesive element of life, or the *dynamis* of the harmonic circulation of human goods according to its intrinsic necessity. Logic, moving in the production and consequent distribution of such goods, is paralyzed, insofar as it is mechanized.

This thinking, insofar as it is dead, cannot grasp the living movement that, as a higher cognitive instinct, provides the economic connection with an immediate impulse—an impulse that, to express itself all the way to the sphere of instincts, must move directly from the spirit. It needs living thinking, namely what once operated as the intuitive–instinctive thinking of the brilliant organizers of production, to whom the most evolved people owe the wellbeing that they are now losing. And it will always be ever more lost, because abstract, noneconomic, but political thought cannot but paralyze the life element of the economic process, or its causal movement, which, in its essentiality, is not graspable by numeric and logical measurement, whose task is only that of interpretative registration and of indication. Similarly, rational thought would paralyze the circulation of the blood, if, through human misfortune, it managed to direct its vital movement.

In reality, at the lowest level, that of the production of economic goods, only the highest thinking can act, which must be free so it does not express itself theoretically but *directly* in sensory data, according to the necessary intuitive connection of concepts that correspond to such data—concepts perceptible respectively in the immediacy of the moving data, thanks to a practical capacity of penetration, which does not undergo ideological constriction.

Those who in the past began to edify the economic organism in certain areas of the Earth—areas from which this economic organism tended to irradiate into the world—were not economic theoreticians or politicians but, rather, practical bearers of economic intuition—the golden race of human labor organizers, which the leveling ideology goes on persecuting and eliminating the world over, under the illusion of targeting in them the egoism proper to the economic praxis, which is actually inherent in the human soul and transformable only within it.

5

FREEDOM

The pure relation, as a pre-dialectical movement, is at the origin of dialectical thought and, thus, of the logical–dialectical relation, which normally loses its essence. But it retains, in accordance with unconscious will, its formal, connective impulse. Such will is the germ of freedom. The formal impulse, in fact, can take on any content. This content, however, lacking an inner connection, cannot overcome the psychic limit, or human–animal subjectivity, instinctiveness.

The logic of the psychic content is that of everyday dialectics, of which we each legitimately make use to contrast our own reasoning to that of others, who have at their disposal a similar formal construct to support their own. Each of us, with our own logic, is quite right; each of us acts in good faith in the struggle against others. But good faith does not eliminate responsibility with respect to the effective inner content.

Nevertheless, we have seen the determination of physical–mathematical thinking be born from pure thinking, the logical relation from the connective power of the pure relation. It is legitimate to think that if the original relation had ruled dialectical thought we would have thought truth automatically. We would not have had a nature opposed to us, because within it we would have felt just as we do within our own bodies. The conflict with another person's truth would not have been possible. Evil would not have existed upon the Earth; yet humans would not have had the possibility of freedom.

Freedom is born at the moment of our opposition to our own nature—primarily to our spiritual nature. It can be said that physical nature is born as a world of forces outside the "I," since the "I" loses it as an inner world, or a spiritual nature. If a paradisiacal state was the original state of human beings, it was undoubtedly a pure relation, like a transcendent virtue, which directs the processes of reality through us. Human beings had to avoid such a transcendent realm to become free.

Only where the power of truth is not restrictive can we begin to feel free—free to edify our own truth. This, however, cannot at first be a partial truth or error. In fact, insofar as we proceed according to the direction of freedom within the most limited aspect of truth (the physical–mathematical one), we undergo conditioning, by means of which the ancient tendency unconsciously resurfaces in us to depend (according to faith) on a principle outside us. At one time, it was a suprasensory necessity; now it is a sensory one. Dependency, once legitimate and the vehicle of the higher power, today becomes a vehicle of the forces adverse to the human being. In reality, modern-day thinking, oblivious to its own autonomy, depends on cerebral mediation. This mediation gives us the opportunity to free ourselves from ancient dependence, but it provides us with a consciousness that is merely reflected. Thinking is free because of such consciousness, but it does not possess freedom, except as a reflected image, therefore, as an expression of corporality, or of the subjective psyche.

Those of us who ignore the dependence on the cerebral mediation lose the conscious determination of thought, which frees itself from the subjective psyche and has a moment of truth in connection with the measurability of the object by willingly connecting itself to the sensory object. Because of such dependence—according to the ancient impulse of non-freedom, or of the submission to revealed truth—we are led to refer to a truth outside us, the world petrified in its *alterity,* the symbol of the lost power of the "I." We are led to believe that truth lies in the outer object, in the quantifiable phenomenon, or in the physical–mathematical formula, and not in the thinking that realizes its immediate inner connection. The sensory object is always a partial aspect of an entity, whose wholeness is provided by thinking. It is the thinking by means of which the "I" begins to recapture its own lost realm—namely, that of being the center of the world's structure.

Freedom is the moment of thinking that moves according to its own principle, realizing it however within the limits given to it by the cerebral mediation, which actually isolates it from the ancient soul but de-realizes it on the dialectical plane. For this reason, there exists no freedom of which we can legitimately speak, prior to thinking's independence from cerebral mediation. The freedom that we believe we find outside of us, in events or outer structures, is nothing but a mirage, because it is always a projection of the psychic vehicle—namely, the vehicle that tends to affirm itself illegitimately as a free impulse. Seekers of freedom must discover that any limit to freedom found outside themselves is a limit that exists within them. Only thinking, or the spirit, can be free. The freedom of a desire, or of an instinct, is the human being's true prison.

Rational thought is not free, yet it possesses the possibility of freedom. It bears, as reflected, the original synthetic power. It possesses it as the moment of independence from the metaphysical relation, but simultaneously as the possibility of independence from the physical relation, which stirs up opposition to the metaphysical. It ignores such a possibility, however, mistaking the reflected impairment for a normal condition. In essence, it occurs as an opposition to the metaphysical source, but, in the reification of the physical alterity, it annihilates the moment of freedom. It ignores the original movement of the relation by making use of it, nonetheless. It draws on a power that remains unknown to it. In fact, it is free, but it does not escape cerebral mediation, which subjects it unconsciously to instincts, or to the human–animal nature.

Reality compels; semblance sets free. We modern human beings, in disregarding metaphysical reality, have an initial moment of freedom, but we do not grasp it, because we do not grasp it where it arises. For this reason, it does not coincide with the moment of reality and of truth. Instead, we turn our backs on metaphysical reality, but, by not knowing thought's dependence on the cerebral mediation, we bind ourselves to physical reality, or to the semblance of reality. This (semblance of reality) does not compel us. It leaves us free, because it enables the limitlessness of subjectivity. We do not take hold of freedom where it arises but, rather, where it becomes estranged, reflectively correlated to the sensory aspect of the "appearing." Therefore, we fail to distinguish the *"appearing"* from the *sensory*.

The life of instincts is correlated to the "appearing." The "appearing" rises by means of the sensory, but as the projection of the original relation, it itself is not sensory. The true suprasensory is the disenchantment of the "appearing," or the overcoming of the reflected state. Sensory consciousness moves from the original relation. However, in being limited to the "appearing," which leaves its subjective being free, it cannot but oppose it. Yet, we possess, within the dimension of freedom, the need of a principle that does not require, for example, either physical or metaphysical support, since it is the original absolute within itself, capable of disenchanting the "appearing" and thus the real physical realm, or real reintegration of instincts. Such instincts control the psyche, there, where reflected thought, believing itself to be free, undergoes cerebral mediation. Indeed, our freedom, as modern-day human beings unconscious of our own inner dependence, is an animal freedom, in which the animal element undergoes corruption, which the animal itself does not know.

Freedom is the moment of thought's pure determination turned to the calculable, or to the logical–dialectical connection. But it is a moment of fleeting life, because, with the connective power transposed to the "appearing," reality is identified with the sensory, and the relation becomes merely quantitative, a shadow or semblance of the original relation.

We are free with regard to the semblance. But we are unable to realize freedom, because we transfer the age-old dependence on inner truth to outer truth. Outer truth, in its quantitative one-dimensionality, leaves us free in all residual activities not engaged in the logic of the sensory realm, but it holds us with the unconscious bond of the ancient faith. Faith is transferred to a palpable fact, to proof. Such obscure faith is, within the present-day human being, the *mental counterpart* of the dependence on instincts. We fail to notice that fact palpates with an inner act. We believe in the product of this inner act, of which we are unaware.

In fact, free thought has its potential moment in the coincidence of the original connectivity with the object's calculable or logical structure, which is not its reality. Thought loses this moment. It thus loses the possibility of an essential reality, since it believes that the relation pertains to the object or to the phenomenon, and not to its own power of synthesis. Thought fails to see within itself the relation that is immediate to it. It transfers this relation outside of itself. It undoubtedly exists within the object, but it is one with its principle, which we can encounter only within the inner life of thought.

Sensory reality is the symbol of the inherent demand of freedom—not half-freedom—or freedom that the contingent (or reflected) "I" appropriates to move freely within its own prison according to dependence on instincts. The sensory object is truly a petition of the liberating action, not of the physical possession, which is the inability to possess it from within. *Physical possession in itself makes no sense.* We become possessed by it; we are not free.

The relation exists within the object, but it is born within think-ing; it is not the object, but only that of it which thought begins to free from alterity. It is the initial identity that should be continued, not itself fixed as alterity, or the initial identity that escapes the thinking that is insufficiently aware of its movement.

The relation belongs to the object, but it has no other seat but consciousness. The relation, born as thought, belongs to the object as much as the sensory characteristics of this (object). By not gathering the relation, the free element of thinking does not gather itself and, thereby, identifies its own moment of freedom with the dialectical form. Thus, it becomes incapable of distin-guishing itself from sensory "mental picturing." The cerebral mediation controls it. By means of the cerebral organ, instincts manage to manipulate it. Thus, it mistakes the instinct's expres-sion for its own free affirmation.

Where the control of reflected consciousness takes place, the instinc-tive current rationally maneuvers the *mechanical* and technological element, thanks to the unconscious identity of the *instinctive* with the *cerebral*. On the other hand, any possible analysis of instinc-tive phenomena cannot but move from the mental realm already controlled by instincts. The impulse of such an investigation could not but be itself identified as an expression of instinctive nature equipped with the most persuasive form, that of rigorous logic.

If one has followed the thread of our considerations with regard to the "forming" of the logical relation as a surrogate for the pure relation, it is easy to realize the possibility for logic to construct the formal edifice of all knowledge that presupposes its own object, assumed as an original datum, simply through its appearing—therefore, without the foundation from which it genuinely moves, or without the recognition of that thinking which, occurring through the sensory, contains the original nucleus of the dialectical process. For this reason, outside a specific ambit of mathematical–physical research, complexes of formally true structures arise as systems of knowledge, but devoid of reality, since they are devoid of original content.

As investigators, we aim to find the pure relation. The initial relation that we experience is one that is logical. We recognize in it the synthetic power of thinking, but reflected. We understand that such power is more important than the synthesis to which it gives rise. The dialectical relation is not the pure relation. Therefore, it is not the power of synthesis, but its inferior projection, the reflection—the support of consciousness conditioned by instincts, or of ephemeral freedom.

Logicians–dialecticians always operate by means of such a projection, ignoring the original synthetic element from which they draw to follow the phenomenon, the formula, the discourse. When they acquire knowledge, they fail to see within themselves the living element of thought set into motion, but they believe they recognize its movement within the thing itself. This (movement) certainly penetrates the thing, but it arises in us as knowledge. It belongs to a thing insofar as it is perceived, but, by unconsciously integrating it, it manifests as its thought. In such a process, which, in its wholeness objectively belongs to reality, the moment of synthesis escapes the logician–dialectician.

Logicians–dialecticians are unaware of seeing what they think about a thing, since they are included in it. They believe that, without such thinking, the thing outside of them is complete—whether they behold a mathematical formula and believe it to contain the element of truth and not the thinking that moves by means of it, or whether they behold an organism and grasp its inner unity, as if this resulted from sensory notes and not from the immediate unifying thinking within them.

Certainly, it is a non-dialectical thinking—intuitive thinking directly within the "perceiving," an immediate and thus unconscious thinking expressive of the same original force that connects concepts as a pure relation—even this (relation) is not normally conscious. It is an immediate power of correlation without which the "perceiving" would be the succession of sensory impressions, devoid of connection.

If this original thinking is recognized, one glimpses the Logos at its source. It is the same force–thought that already contains within itself the unity of being. Therefore, in its immediate "identifying" with being, in the pre-dialectical moment of thinking and of perceiving, it does not know duality. But this immediate identifying is unconscious. It becomes conscious at the cost of the cerebral mediation and thus of being reflected by means of this (mediation), until it becomes an *"appearing"* of thinking, which ceases to *be*. It is an appearing that still has within it the power of identity, but only to coincide with the "appearing" of the world—namely, *maya* that does not constrain but leaves us free, estranged from the authority of the spirit but also from "being" as the being of thought—free, but fallen into dual vision, and free but devoid of the formative force regarding the substance of our very being, for which matter escapes us and we see it outside of ourselves.

It is, therefore, thought that has the same physical corporality outside of it and, therefore, also sees apart from itself the "perceiving," whose unconscious living element is, instead, one with the world. Thus, there exists the unusual contradiction of identifying with a reality that it has expelled from itself, losing it as the life of its unity; conferring to it—insofar as it is dualized and opposite—the successive chrism of the reflected identity, or of the illusory unity.

The world that exists on its own thus emerges, without the Logos—the strongest appearance, the everyday hallucination confirmed by the fact that this outer reality exists; it has its ironclad logic. It conditions us. It arrests us. It enchants us. It overwhelms us. It becomes an obstacle for us. Yet, with this, it stimulates our knowing. It paralyzes our knowing, but it leads this knowing to a dead end of the whole mechanism, which knowing is obliged to overcome so as not to cease being the sense of life; so as to find within itself—opposite the error and the continuous inevitable counterfeiting of truth—the pure relation, namely the movement that for now it knows how to see only outside of itself. In truth, we can perceive the movement in virtue of what moves within us independently of corporality.

❧

Owing to spiritual practice, one can glimpse the pure relation as the *light of life* of thinking—an original movement that bears within itself the unity of the world, the inner synthetic power of the concept and, likewise, the immediate life of thinking within "perceiving." We have been able to touch on an indicative hypothesis. That is to say, if the pure relation controlled thinking, we would completely realize truth; we would not know error, nor consequently evil, but we would not be free. Each of us would be an impeccable spiritual automaton, namely that to which, today, certain mystagogues and kabbalists belatedly tend without hope, unconsciously opposing the secret impulse of the Logos on Earth.

It is obvious that we have lost the original synthetic power so we can know—opposite the dual world and its alternative—the dimension of freedom to recapture later, on the basis of free individuality, the original synthetic power. But such an undertaking demands the correlative guiding knowledge, or its esotericism, so as not to fail, given that the preliminary process of freedom takes place for us in accordance with a de-spiritualized vision of things, that of the mineral "appearing," at a level in which duality separates subject from object, thought from life, substance from form.

It is a rhetorical freedom, devoid of the vital lymph, because it emerges from reflected thought's adherence to the alterity, for which the physical world illegitimately acquires a power of reality, which constitutes a limit to the spirit that is not awake, namely *a limit that maneuvers freedom*. Reflected thought, adhering to cerebralism, cannot distinguish itself from physiological nature. This physiological nature, although one with the outer physical world within itself, is felt dually in this respect as the world of subjectivity in relation to the one opposite to objectivity.

Longing is the relation of nature divided within its very self. This longing could lose its power over us only if our thinking, by virtue of the original synthetic moment, attained the identity with itself and therefore the transcendent unity at the foundation of the world, and realized the inner human being to be one with the Logos, namely with the world, beyond the appearing of this world as physical multiplicity. The human again becomes one with the world by means of the thinking that gives itself to the world, emerging by way of the sensory realm. But it is precisely the dialectical arrest of this thinking that paralyzes the initial force and generates duality—the contradiction that feeds desire.

We behold the world and think it with the thinking that we bear within us, but we ignore the original synthetic impulse. The form in which the world arises from this beholding and thinking begins to be the overcoming of duality. It is the initial reconstitution of the original unity, albeit in a one-dimensional sensory form. But for this reconstitution to continue, it must be recognized. We need to cognize the *extrasensory movement* by means of which we begin to operate within the sensory. This movement is the immediate life of meditating.

In truth, we can follow what, within the world, moves outside us, given that we unconsciously experience the movement within our own etheric body. The fact that we can see matter move and the movement unfold externally, on its own, is an error, since the etheric correlation escapes us—the correlation that renders the movement and its perception simultaneously possible, the inner movement of every existing thing. Those of us who are unaware of this movement within ourselves cannot gain true meditation, the path of freedom, because we are united with the world by means of a force that escapes us. In truth, matter does not move. It is moved.

6

THE SECRET OF MATTER

Dialectical freedom is the symbol of freedom. It is not freedom. Unaware of being free within the semblance of thinking and in relation to the semblance of reality, rather than within thinking, we, by means of the logic of semblance, which is dialectics, can codify our own subjection to material necessity. The cerebral mediation necessary to the dialectical moment controls the process of which it should simply be the vehicle. Rather than as an instrument of thinking, the cerebral organ operates as an organ of the nervous system, or of the human's animal structure, of the psyche. The series of sensations, of impressions and of instinctive impulses, maneuvers thought, given that it is dialectical thought, devoid of life. The animal human enslaves the spiritual human.

Despite believing ourselves to be free, we, as dialectical human beings, cannot help but think according to our own physical nature, because of thinking's dependence on the cerebral organ. We do not know the moment of thinking's independence from such an organ. We do not know the original synthetic power of thinking in which the spirit lives, namely the power of life, which flows from the system of forces that operates independently of *karma*, but undergoes *karma* there, where thinking is subjected by means of cerebralism to a determined sentient nature. They are forces that, by penetrating the sensory, structurally control the physical organism, as formative forces—the forces of form at all levels of matter. Thanks to the volitional union with these forces, thinking again becomes living. Moreover, it ceases to be thought, so as to rise again as a creative force.

The task of the human being that thinks is unique in the universe. In the encounter of the "I" with the astral body, thought rises as a "light of fire," which burns in accordance with the flow of free individual willing. Dialectical intelligence is the pale reflection of this light of fire. Only we humans are free to think what we want. The thinking of the Gods is always identical to its own perfection. The task of the initiate is to perceive the light of the fire that lights up, thanks to the moment of freedom, in original thinking. This perception demands overcoming the dialectical level, which is thinking conditioned by physical materiality.

For as much as dialectical thought is the de-realization of original thinking, it nonetheless draws unconsciously from such thinking. It draws the logical relational movement from it, just as it draws the sense of reality from the extrasensory element of perception. Notwithstanding the dependence on the cerebral mediation, thought in ordinary "perceiving–mental picturing" begins to lift itself from reflectivity, or from duality, by constantly leading the matter it encounters back to an *inner form*. But it ignores this. In such a form, it initiates, minimally, embryonically, the reunification of what has been separated. It tends to perceive its own fire of light. In reality, at the sensory level the spirit's most powerful forces operate, or those by means of which the spiritual human becomes an earthly human. They are the forces that contemporary traditional esotericism tends to ignore. Meanwhile, they constitute the *"materia prima"* (raw material) of the work.

The conscious investigator further develops the embryonic reunification until perceiving the current of living light that unites with the warmth reawakened from minerality in the sensory experience. To begin with, we must know what, on the suprasensory plane, takes place within us when we perceive and picture the world to ourselves. We can achieve this by penetrating the processes by means of which we perceive and think, until knowing the forces that express themselves through such processes, independently of their object.

No matter moves on its own. Instead, there exists only a *movement* that operates by means of matter, beyond it, in spite of it, by overcoming its gravity. Such movement is immaterial. It is the etheric dynamic of the world, which has its synthesis in our etheric bodies, and is at the heart of all perceiving and thinking. However, we lack the sufficient forces of consciousness to perceive within ourselves the etheric relation, surfacing minimally in perceiving–thinking, which connects us to the world. We believe that the world exists outside us, as (something) other, objective, isolated, waiting to be known.

Matter continues to exist as alterity, beyond "perceiving–mental picturing," because this is continuously deprived, by reflected thinking, of the original element of the identity. The initial identity cannot be recognized, without *ulterior* forces of consciousness, or the original forces capable of overcoming the level of reflectivity.

Non-recognition of the identity at the source of each "knowing" leads to the illusory impression that the world, as it appears, is such beyond "perceiving" and "mental picturing." This impression, in turn, determines our attitude with respect to our own interiority. The original interiority has no authority over us. It descends within us only as a mediated power. We are free. We are not obligated by metaphysical certainty but, rather, only by *physical certainty,* which, however, is contingent, insofar as it is correlated to the appearing—i.e., to the physical measurability of reality. This measurability, while it binds us to the sensory level, leaves us free at every other level—moral, psychological, spiritual—but free only to logically justify any choice at the level of the measurable, a choice that cannot but be determined by instincts.

Interiority, by not coinciding with the original moment of the reflected determination, which, as we have seen, is a moment of independence from the subjective psyche, inevitably coincides with the product of the determination, at the psychic or psychophysical level. Such a product, even itself, actually unfolds as an *extra-animic,* or *a-psychic,* process, but within the astral–animal or psychic realm, deprived of the spiritual element from which the determination arises. Therefore, our virtual freedom expresses its mobility within the prison of matter's "appearing." We continuously draw from the spiritual an element of freedom, which, because of the inability of the reflected determination to identify with the spiritual content, necessarily identifies with the sentient content, that is, with instinct. The *human* coincides with the *human–animal.*

We are free today because we are not obligated by suprasensory certainties—those we form insofar as they correlate to appearance. Such certainties do not obligate us, but we ignore the relation that they have with appearance. The relation springs from our inner being, as a pure intuitive moment, unseen and unconscious. We continuously lose such a moment and, with it, we lose the beginning of the identity with the world, which nonetheless rises before us thanks to the initial identity. Due to the alienation of this (identity), the world arises before us as alterity opposed to us. But it is truly opposite our animal consciousness. Matter exists in relation to such consciousness.

Conditioned freedom is born from the opposition as the germ of a freedom that we cannot realize within the sphere of duality. In fact, as much as the inner act is in itself independent, it nonetheless leans on the alterity. It depends on the psyche, or on sentient (or animal) nature. This freedom is born as an opposition to the spiritual. It is born as a negation of the suprasensory in the mathematical–physical, or quantitative, correlation with the sensory. But its germinal point, as we have shown, is the pure moment of the determination—a moment from which the initial power of identity of the "I" with the world emerges. This original moment is quickly lost, but remains as an inner impulse turned toward the sensory and, thus, de-realized, which equally utilizes the soul's forces for its own expression at that level. It needs sensory support, since it lacks the possibility of beholding itself as a pure support, namely, as a foundation. But it does not know how to be conscious of itself as an original moment, a power of identity with the sensory.

The spiritual practitioner must discover this original moment, because only it has the power to overcome the barrier of matter that confines us within the human–animal (state). This primordial element, which sleepy spiritualists seek within doctrines, within myths and within the symbols of the past, is the present princi-ple, the "light's lightning bolt" of the "I," which surfaces as secret, essential, but ignored, in "fallen" thinking. Inconceivable to mate-rialists, avoided by spiritualists (both actually identified with their dialectics), it is the adamantine thread that connects the soul to its center of perpetuity. Therefore, it bears the power of overcoming the enchantment of matter, all the way to the level in which the soul can decidedly will it.

It is this will that, within reflected thought's vehicle of logic, can turn to the origin of reflectivity. Just as thought is the light fallen into reflectivity, matter is the light fallen and solidified into the state of physicality. Thought, logically dialectical, can perceive the essen-tial logicality of reconnecting with its own imaginative–instinctive current and opening itself up to the living principle of light that gives it logical movement. Logical movement is the sign of the light, or its indication. Yet, with respect to the creative power, it is nothing.

In fact, as it has been shown, the "I" cannot live within reflected thought. The dialectical "I" is essentially an "I" whose existence can legitimately be put into question. It is a reflected "I," which we can discuss by means of unlimited dialectics, without minimally penetrating its reality. Therefore, we cannot penetrate the inside of a thought, or of a sentiment, or of an impulse. We cannot enter anything. We must limit ourselves to the superficial measurement of everything and, behind the surface, feel the reality of matter. We must coexist with the chaos of psychophysical life, by limiting ourselves to a peripheral, pellicular and quantitative, or dialectical control of it. We do not truly operate from the center of ourselves, from the "I." We cannot penetrate the "profound," because we believe in an internal weaving of matter. This interior is its interiority, which we do not know how to penetrate.

Instead, within imaginative–intuitive thinking lives the "I," the meaning of the history of the human being resumes. We can comprehend the sense of our imprisonment within the sensory, which keeps us from penetrating the sensory world. We still have not truly entered the sensory. The source of our error, the origin of evil, is to desire the sensory, feeling ourselves to be outside of it, whereas we are actually within it, though without the sufficient forces of consciousness to notice it. Dialectical consciousness separates us from our own profound reality, which is the depth of our being inserted within the physical–sensory (realm).

The intuitive–imaginative current from which thinking—to the extent that it is free—can draw, does not have the sensory world opposite it, or a *substance* to know as alterity, because it contains the sensory within itself. There exists no matter that opposes such a current.

Matter is not opposed to the light but, rather, to the reflection of the light, or to reflected thought. "The light shines in the darkness." Actually, the darkness is the inverse light that emanates from matter. Thanks to sensory perceiving, time after time the rising of material alterity in forms and colors is the initial resurging of the light from matter. In fact, there is no sensory perception in which the light of pre-dialectical thinking is not present. The world's colors are a sign of the light's struggle with the darkness. Each color is the level of the light's victory over the obscurity of matter, from which the original substance of the light begins to free itself, thanks to the percipient and thinking human being.

Our task on Earth is to resurrect the light that lies lifeless within matter. Thinking actually becomes lifeless so it can connect with matter. Leaving aside the stultification of matter to which the nuclear theoreticism today arrives, even if abstract, we must say that matter does not exist outside the human being, except to the degree in which, by means of perceiving and of thinking, consciousness, estranged from its own formative light, needs a sensory support to exist. Human beings, prior to the "fall" within sensory limits, had an available soul life that did not require individual form to irradiate, since it is itself the same form developed by the cosmic powers of light.

Matter became alterity as a support necessary to the fallen soul, which moves toward the conquest of its own form, or of the conscious element of the light. The suprasensory forces that operate within the depths of the corporeal structure of the soul's support are the most powerful that the spiritual practitioner is given to know through the liberation of the conscious principle. By "perceiving–mental picturing," the disciple begins to glimpse such forces, to the extent that they give rise to matter within the *form*. This form is actually *internal*. It is the resurrection of the light.

Inner form is the three-dimensional space in which this matter appears situated; the inner form is its "appearing," just like any relation between one point of it and another. When we think the inside of matter, we do not notice that we think its inner volume at whose surface its form would come up again anew if we penetrated such an interior. We think the internal form of matter. We have no other way to begin penetrating it, to overcome its unreal alterity. In truth, it is not material "experimenting" that thinking relies upon as an instrument, but thinking itself, which can directly penetrate the structure of matter, insofar as it realizes, within itself, the form by means of which it encounters this structure.

Sensory perception is the world's datum of material form, but this datum, in being perceived, is already removed from materiality. No other matter exists beyond that relating to the perceptible, which is the datum where the overcoming of alterity begins. Matter beyond the perceptible is the alterity imaginatively reproduced and added to the perceived by weak, dialectical thinking.

For this weak thinking, matter is true; and so justifiably this thinking must explore it, just like wanderers pursue their shadow, which one cannot deny is true, even if it lacks reality in itself. Wanderers will pursue their own shadow until they become aware of being its projector and discover themselves. Thus, reflected thought, the shadow of the light of thinking, by establishing itself as a value in its dead discursiveness or shadowiness, will always oppose living thinking. It will always tend to keep its alienation safe and sound with respect to it, because in this alienation the dual vision that it needs, exists. Matter will mystically continue to exist. Reality will continue to be the object of investigation, or (the object) of a form that will never grasp anything of it, no matter how infinitesimally it examines it in a mathematical–physical sense.

The process of reflected thinking is possible only provided that the death of living thinking continuously takes place. It has been possible for us to observe that if living thinking controlled the mental sphere, we would be one with the reality of the world. We would not know error. We would not know separation. We would not know evil, nor would we know death, because the inexhaustible current of life would not find an interruption in the organ by means of which consciousness emerges, as sensory consciousness, that is to say, as consciousness that cannot but emerge on the dual plane of opposition. On such a plane, in fact, the mental sphere opposes living thinking. The sensory is identified with what appears, given that it is devoid of what sustains it—the suprasensory. For this reason, reflected thinking will always seek this (suprasensory) beyond or behind the phenomena of matter. Meanwhile, the suprasensory is the dimension from which reflected thinking (within its inner depths) continuously draws and simultaneously estranges itself.

That matter moves or evolves is the tragic "error of thought" of the obtuse, but dialectical and logical human being. It is superstition, blunder, and obscure faith. In truth, matter opposes movement. It resists and contradicts all evolution. It is the symbol of death. It evolves only if it dies to itself, if it disintegrates or is annihilated by the super-material powers that rule it, and that, by inverting its inner polarity, edify life by means of it.

Matter is the petrification of an original thinking, whose power, the fallen human being, at a given moment, has not been capable of thinking. Matter, in that sense, is a symbol. It is not a reality. It is the past, or creation fallen outside the original force, outside the force by means of which original thinking used to think it. The spiritual practitioner of the new times, or the solar spiritual practitioner, is the one who recognizes the initial reawakening of the force of thinking's free self-movement, independent of the past. In ordinary "perceiving–mental picturing," we recognize the embryonic inner act that is the beginning of the de-crystallization of matter. There exists no hardening that, perceived and thought, does not already begin to be overcome.

Matter is actually the inverse light, solidified, which the light of living thinking can reawaken. This is the real movement of matter, for which it is grasped and recreated in living nature by universal thinking, according to specific archetypes.

Matter exists, undoubtedly, but as a world that arises through sensory perception, a perception that does not manifest but by means of a subject that immediately imbues it with inner content, in which the force of the *form* of *matter* is in progress. Matter, existing in itself outside such a formal process, or outside the percipient subject and its inner act within matter, does not exist unless it is thought, or imagined and added to what is already perceived. In reality, what is perceived is everything, insofar as it is sufficient unto itself. Matter exists, but one should be forewarned that it exists where it is perceived and not beyond. It does not have an "inner" of its own, or a "profound." The profundity is always an inner dimension, or a relation of thought. One must be careful not to make a mythical entity, or a modern, dialectical, logical superstition out of matter.

The hardening of matter is a symbol of the solar undertaking of thought, which begins thanks to the forces that thinking develops by sinking into the sphere of the senses. Our cognitive act is partially engaged in perception. It partially surfaces as mental image and concept. Such an act belongs to reality, not any less than matter and the energy proper to the sensory structure. Thought or the concept constitutes, above all, a pre-dialectical unity with the object to which it refers. Such unity, however, is not conscious. The spiritual practitioner has the task of realizing it. The reality of the physical phenomenon includes, with the same inevitability, its sensory manifesting and its intuitive content. The phenomenon's greater or lesser capacity of penetration depends on the possibility of being aware of such content.

Thought belongs to reality, a reality that appears to manifest because of its *being.* On the other hand, already present within this being is thought, namely, the most powerful thought, as the *force of the form* of matter. It is not rational or dialectical thinking, but thinking that, as a force, is identical to being. This identity and this force are unknown. The spiritual practitioner experientially understands that this thinking, as an immediate pure force, has the power to penetrate matter directly, more so than a physical experience, which is arrested at the point of abstract quantity, the temporary vehicle of thinking unaware of its "being–force."

In being part of reality, thinking is living, but not conscious. There, where it emerges in a conscious state, it is dialectical and lifeless. For this reason, it deadens or paralyzes into abstract materiality the physical reality in whose form it unconsciously cooperates. Thinking that attains this level of inner life through discipline— essentially, by turning to things—has their inner life up to that level. It reanimates the world.

The discipline of such thinking consists in overcoming the materiality within itself, namely not only a dependence on the physical support, but also the formal impression of this support. Thinking realizes the formal power as its own so that it can exist according to its own foundation. It can realize that inner life, which does not need corporeal support to exist. In fact, the more it makes itself independent of it, the more its formative power manifests. The inner life of thinking is also present within immediate perception. Our unawareness of it makes the material world appear opposed, lifeless, and dual to us.

The deadening of thought, from which ensues the deadening of the world, has come about for a positive function, liberating the soul from the ancient inner world nowadays devoid of the living spiritual element that nevertheless survives in superstitious impulses. The deadening of thought requires that we draw inner life from thinking's pure relation with sensory materiality, not from the psyche. A task of purifying the conscious spiritual element is connected to the concrete experience of the sensory (realm). The subsequent form of such a task is not to add soul to the materiality that is investigated but, rather, to overcome the initial abstractness of the cognitive act through the awareness of realized thought, in which new soul life is urgently needed. Such consciousness wards off each unconscious mystical representation that tends to unite freely with perception. It gathers the spirit's *pure presence* in the thinking that permeates perception.

Thinking forms part of the reality that appears physical and, there, where it is present by means of perception, it expresses its utmost life. We, however, are not conscious in living thinking but, rather, in reflected or lifeless thought. Nevertheless, without the non-dialectical current of thinking by means of the sense organs, that immersion into the sensory, thanks to which thinking expresses its maximum force, would not be possible. Such a force, which the spiritual practice of thinking has the task of identifying, is normally unconscious.

Perception is a living experience, whose content of life nevertheless takes place at the level of sleep and dream consciousness. We who consciously achieve such levels of consciousness would have the integral experience of reality. We would know the secret of the three-dimensional world. We continuously penetrate this secret by means of perception, but in an unconscious state. This unconscious state is the limit of dialectical consciousness, which accordingly has the material world outside of it and subordinates thought to its alterity, losing the spiritual meaning of its immersion in the sensory.

Knowing should be the conscious realization of what perception already possesses at the level of sleep or of dream consciousness. Today, the scientist permeated with positivism, aspires to remain at the experience's pure datum, without adding anything personal to it. But this is not possible for us as long as we manipulate a fact of which we are not conscious. In perceiving, we indeed have the sensory datum, but simultaneously inserted within it, (we have) the internal datum, which rises before us as a concept. Yet, we ignore it. We ignore the initial "overcoming" that we actualize of duality. In reality, thinking manifests to us just like the sensory object. The concept that we form of an object, or of a phenomenon, is the attempt to reconstitute the inner content, present within perception, by means of conscious thinking.

It is this content, which, thanks to perception, normally gives the impression of being before reality. But we make the mistake of considering this reality to be founded upon itself and to be opposite thinking and, therefore, in need of being known, as such. Meanwhile, knowing has already begun within perception. Spatial–temporal sensory processes are essential to the structure of perception, but this perception is held together by an inner content that constitutes the essence of such processes. The mathematical-physical measurement of an object, in fact, lacks such content. The mathematical–physical content can hardly reconstitute it. Only a *higher* use of such content can make it a vehicle of the awareness of the essential content.

Such an achievement is connected to the possibility that the seeker realizes, within the experience, the liberation of the principle of consciousness that experiences, or of the "I." From an absolute point of view, the experience of matter has an ascetic and purifying function. By means of it, we can notice that, just as the sensory world reveals itself to us thanks to the pure movement of perception, the corresponding thought manifests to us with the same pure movement. Thought manifests to us objectively, just like the sensory content. The experience of this "manifesting" of thought within the "perceiving" is the true sense of sensory knowledge. It leads the research beyond the limit at which science has been arrested.

The consciousness of thinking, as a fact that is as objective as that provided by the sensory world, directs us (as investigators) to the *animadversio* (observation) of the original thinking that manifests itself to us, but within perception. Yet, it is simultaneously the original nucleus of the concept. The concept, in effect, overcomes matter.

Therefore, we cannot deduce the existence of matter from sensory experience. As an entity, which, in itself, exists beyond the form in which it is perceived, we indeed have such matter (if we observe well enough) only as an unconscious mental image. Sensory reality is true, but matter that is at the heart of it as a universal, complete in itself, is an idea, unaware of being an idea and, therefore unaware of its own objective content—a mental image that, as such, is unconscious. It is the mental image of a *quid* that, through an absence of the pre-dialectical element of perception to which it refers, illegitimately places itself behind the forms, the colors, the sizes and the sounds of things, as a free-standing substratum. Such phenomena are true, but matter that exists underneath and behind, is merely a naïve representation—namely, subconscious nourishment of the modern idolatry of matter.

If the matter to which we allude exists as an internal structure, we have to wonder to which other type of perception must we resort to perceive it, beyond the aspect of it that manifests as form, size color, sound, and so on in ordinary perceptions, which is the only sensory being of which we have the right to speak. It is the only sensory being that, if we are clearheaded and honest, arises as an objective perceptive relationship—an encounter, a pre-dialectical synthesis, an identity of the "I" with the thing perceived, which is the whole perceptive process, behind which it is absurd to add something that lies behind. Because *behind or underneath*, there is nothing other than *the same*, which is already perceived.

7

SPACE AND THE FLASH OF THE LOGOS

The perception of the living content of perception gives us, as researchers, a way to experience the living element closed to reflected consciousness, which nevertheless has it nearby, alongside, but it does not know where. And it secretly intuits it and believes that it grasps it, but again and again, it feels it slipping away into sensation.

The experience of the living content of perception allows us to know the secret of the three dimensions. Of these, only one is sensory. The other two are internal, as suprasensory structural relations of the first, constituting its previously mentioned living content. The volume is the inner form of matter, born out of the need for consciousness to relate the various points of space to the essential constitutional order. If length as a linear distance is the immediate relation between one point and another at the sensory level, width as a surface is already the internal relation between two lengths; and height, or depth, as volume, is the internal relation between two surfaces.

Space is born from the spontaneous but unconscious *inner synthesis* of the three dimensions. Outside the internal relation of sensory points, according to the threefold relation mentioned, the concept of physical space is unsustainable. One imagines that the sensory points of reference disappear; that is to say, space appears as a great void, but such a great void would be physically imperceptible. One would need to return to the internal datum of sensory perceiving to have a real sense of space.

The living element that bursts into the inorganic (realm) and grasps material substances to edify life, surfaces as an internal content within perception, namely a content that secretly coincides with the structural movement of bodies, according to their general mold. The perception of a mineral is distinguished from that of a plant because the non-dialectical living element in the perception of the mineral is intuited free of the physicality in which it leaves its own cosmic imprint. In the plant, one sees it engaged in inner spatiality, according to an extraterrestrial structural rhythm, which obeys a terrestrial *necessity*.

In the living forms of earthliness, the spirit conforms to this necessity. It descends there on condition of adapting itself to the laws of the physical manifestation. This necessity also conditions the internal forces that are later incarnated for the animal and human structure. The human "I" cannot but contradict such a necessity, since the spirit is free outside of it and, nonetheless, operative within it. The inner life of the human being—animic and spiritual—is but minimally incarnated, but not even disincarnated, like it is in its sublime, but reflected, suprasensory reality. However, in being reflected, despite bearing the overcoming of nature's necessity, it undergoes this necessity. And this is the sense of its ephemeral freedom.

Nonetheless, we have seen that there is a moment of the spirit's *incarnation* in the pre-dialectical flash of thinking, just as there is in the essential content of perception. Whoever could experience this moment of the spirit's incarnation would have the secret of life, which, from the spirit's a-dimensional world, enters the three-dimensional world.

Regarding inorganic materiality, the ideal weft of the dimensions with respect to the physical condition is evident, which is the only one that is sensory and, therefore, referable to only one of the three dimensions. The other two, the second and third, are suprasensory. Yet, even the first, as a relation from one point of space to another, is suprasensory, insofar as it is a relation of thought. Nevertheless, it is the only one to express a sensory value. The second and third dimensions integrate it, since they correspond to the threefold necessity of relation that we unconsciously bear within our own inner life, with respect to the physical dimension. Such inner life expresses itself as physical experience, but it simultaneously arises as a mental image and a concept.

The relationship changes with respect to the living being, because within this kingdom the dimensional relation is carried within the structure of the bodies. With regard to the appearance of the inorganic (realm), the three-dimensional relation is a pre-dialectical act of thinking, mediated by sensory perception. Instead, in the living being, the relation unconsciously coincides with an inner structural process. It is true that living entities, plants, animals and human beings exist in three-dimensional space, as do lifeless entities. But what is the outer texture of space for inanimate entities, in animate entities nevertheless moves from an imperceptible and a-spatial void as an edifying process. The living being is the expression of the spiritual dimension that permeates the other two dimensions all the way to physicality.

In the living being, we can gather the lightning element of the spirit, which, from its emptiness, shatters the enchantment of matter, unifying the outer multiplicity, by means of a potential for extinction and for re-edification of materiality—which actualizes an archetypal order as form. Such suprasensory potential, as a dynamic weaving of space, penetrates space, or the internal ambit of entities, which, for now, we penetrate only intuitively. We actually conceive space as an ideal relation between one sensory point and another, but unconsciously identify it with outer objectivity. In reality, this outer objectivity, by means of fallen thought, precedes the appearing of space, or apparent space.

By means of the living body, the extra-spatial movement of life and of the light of life enters apparent space. Such a movement operates as an irresistible power of a *void* that gradually, by drawing from the essence, becomes a void that is more than a void, until it devours matter and recreates it under its symbol, the archetype. For its part, human thought is possible through a void produced by the moment of the thinking determination thanks to a destructive process of the organic cerebral life. Creative thinking, which edifies the living being, demands a "void more than the void," by means of which it annihilates and reshapes matter from within to edify the form of life.

The element of the spirit, because of its *radiant quality,* does not descend in its entirety, which would burn up life. Such life, as earthly life, takes part in nature, rather than in supra-nature, by tending to maintain, at the sentient level, the animal structure as a defense against the spiritual. The "lightning flash" element comes from supra-nature and surfaces (reflected by consciousness) as thought. It is the thinking that, nonetheless, in its emerging moment, is the intuitive power of the process for which the spirit becomes Nature, by binding itself to vital and vital–animal conditions. The "lightning flash" element surfaces in us on condition of *destroying,* within us, what tends to express, as nature edified by the spirit, its own "vitality–animal" in spiritual form.

The birth of the spirit within us occurs at the price of the death of what lives within us according to terrestrial necessity. Ancient spiritual paths were for ascetics, who inwardly tended not to lose the connection of earthly human necessity with the Divine, by regulating it as an inferior manifestation of the Divine, so as to prevent human nature from being overcome by earthly currents. But we had to undertake earthly experience, for which the whole story originated based on the drama of losing the primordial Logos. We had to undertake the experience of earthliness until conquering egoic consciousness and the freedom correlated to the vision of the world devoid of the Divine, or of the Logos.

Once present-day disciples of the spirit, through the conscious use of the principle of freedom, recognize the suprasensory structure of the world and of their own psychophysiological nature, they discover that the spirit can *repermeate* this nature only by destroying it and rebuilding it. They will not commit themselves to the methods of yoga and of past wisdom or of their modern adaptations, which tend to continue the relationship once mediated by irregular entities ruled by celestial hierarchies, thanks to the traditional ritual—a relationship actually expired. Instead, they will follow the method of the new times, to which immediate thinking, powerful in its immediacy, intensified to the point of becoming conscious, opens the passage. Such thinking is realized through an opposition to ancient natural formative processes and to the destruction of the vital–physical element, both needed to produce a *void* to the flow of the pure forces of the "I." The spiritual practice of the new times enables the investigator to willfully deepen this process of destruction of the vital nature, thereby radicalizing the "void" and opening the threshold to the re-edifying spirit.

The thinking taking place in concentration (liberated thinking) is still human thinking, which draws its own force from its opposition to the nature "abandoned by the Divine." At this level, it develops as an inner suprasensory movement, the impulse of freedom, but it must overcome this level to realize freedom. It must overcome the animal–human limit to restore to Nature the connection with the lost principle. It can retrace the cosmic dimension of the fall into matter, insofar as it connects (within itself) to the inner *cosmic Impulse*, namely to the principle from which Nature has become alienated.

True spiritual practice is what enables the Logos flash of lightning to *strike* the vital–animal nature, which tends to keep its own psychophysiological processes intact, where the necessity of death is really introduced. The vital–animal nature is not to be supplied with spiritual powers but, rather, transformed. This transformation, when authentic, is essentially a process of destruction and re-edification. The spiritual process, which connects the material dimension in the living being with the archetypal edifying power—for which the second and third dimensions constitute the internal suprasensory relation of matter—is essentially that process of matter's disintegration reintegration, which manifests as life. The disintegration and the reintegration of matter is the prerequisite of the process of life. Matter, as we were able to consider in the preceding chapter, is light solidified in its denying of itself. Each disintegration of matter is a moment of re-ascension of the light, physically imperceptible.

The human "I," like self-consciousness and freedom, becomes the bearer of this process of disintegration and reintegration, indicating within itself a direction opposite to that of the vital–physical nature, which attracts the light of the spirit to itself for its own animal–vital processes. The "I" within the vehicle of *pure thinking* inverts such a direction and tends to destroy those processes. It goes against the vital–physical nature, not to bind itself to it and undergo even the deception of its yogic–mediumistic self-empowering as egoic–animal nature, but to destroy it and rebuild it according to the spirit.

It is a destruction–re-edification that is gradually carried out by means of the spiritual practice of thinking. As an ordinary mental process, thinking is in itself the initial death process of ancient spiritual–animal nature. It is simultaneously a process of death and the *disappearance* of matter. In addition to being a destroyer, thought becomes a rebuilder, when, by insisting on being drawn from its own original light, it reproduces within itself the process by means of which the Logos edifies life. Thought can discover the life of its own light in its own pre-dialectical moment, as well as in the non-dialectical content of perception. The resolution of matter is, at first, a logical fact. This logical fact must become inner experience. In that way, it coincides with the splendor of the Logos, which annihilates the obscurity of human nature.

Obscurity determines the ethical level of human culture and socioeconomic processes, which manifest according to a systematic nature justified by the theoretic ends that are pursued—namely, a system of ironclad necessity with regard to which there is, nevertheless, no transformation that does not have to occur secretly by virtue of a destructive, re-edifying current, in an absolutely inner sense, according to the impulse of the Logos, which alone resolves the kingdom of matter and of its dialectics, which is the kingdom of death.

The art of the spiritual practitioner is to connect with what is absolutely new on Earth and which rules earthliness precisely because it does not belong to the Earth. The "new," to which the "revolutionaries" of today aspire—but not so much, however, as not to unconsciously serve a conservative process, in its outer mechanism—is precisely this. All that is human within the human being, is that for which the human being proceeds toward death. The impulse that restores life to the human annihilates the human by means of which the *ego* lives, which jealously guards ancient nature with its human–animal ambitions, whether revolutionary or conservative.

The impulse restorer of life does not belong to the Earth, because it is more than the Earth, as its transcendent foundation and, therefore, also as the principle independent of it. Its kingdom "is not of this world," because the world as dead earthliness is only a shadow of its real domain, which truly contains the world beyond its state of death.

Each person has, as a secret petition of life, the overcoming of the human being's obscurity, which is the earthliness involving death. We seek the Logos because, obscurely, we seek the principle that delivers us from evil, from error and from destruction, but we cannot find it as long as we ignore our own "I," which bears the force of the Logos within it. The birth of the "I" as self-consciousness, in modern times, has no other purpose—namely, not to be bound to

psychophysiological nature, not to become a kind of epiphenom-
enon of it but, rather, to achieve independence from it, to move from
one's own suprasensory foundation or from the principle that has
the power to destroy and re-edify life.

8

CHRIST WITHIN THOUGHT

The spiritual practitioner perceives the intuitive–imaginative current as an inner reality of all that of the world which appears
external. It is the Logos that cannot have the world opposite it,
because it has got it within itself. Our task as spiritual practitioners
is to realize such a possibility. We are separated from the Logos in
reflected thought, but within the original forces of thought, we are
free to incarnate it, so as to be able one day to incarnate it completely within the soul, all the way to the organic will; all the way
to mineral corporality.

That the Logos descends from the Father and that the Logos
becomes flesh is the image of an event to which the transcendent
process of thinking—rather than of feeling or of the will—is connected in modern times. Yet, historically, in the preparatory phase
of such a process, feeling and the will (according to the persistence
of an original impulse) alone possess the power of communion with
the Logos on Earth. The first "initiatory" Christianity, in fact, only
mystically intuited the Logos. It is the intuitive power that will
immediately spring into action within consciousness, when it enliv-
ens the rational thought that occurs in the sensory (realm) for the
edification of the natural science.

As this intuitive movement is gradually transferred to thinking
consciousness, the sentient, affective soul—or ancient, mystical
soul—is deprived of it. The intuition of the Logos can no longer

have feeling as its seat, since its immediate vehicle is thinking. This intuition, itself, becomes thought's pre-dialectical power of identity, namely a pure power of the will. This means, however, that, to the degree in which current thinking is not conscious of its inner power of identity and does not consequently realize the logic of its own movement, the inverse of the reflected movement, the intuitive source of the Logos dries up within the soul. In reality, feeling and willing are *waiting* to be reconnected to the Logos through the redemption of thought.

As much as traditions and religions painfully force themselves to rekindle the content of the revelation and of the mysteries through revived ritualistic forms and new dogmas, nothing essentially functions any longer. Reflected consciousness lacks the living element. With the spiritual mystically revived through the help of the Kabbalah and hermetic–alchemical symbols, yoga, occultism, and magic do not escape the sphere of feeling that undergoes the captivity of reflected thought. Essentially operating behind the revivification of traditional spiritualism is the impulse that tends to impede the living experience of the Logos. The lifeless (or cadaveric) can only move mechanically, or on condition of submitting itself to the logical *dynamis* of quantity, by means of outer, ceremonial, dialectical, psychophysiological dead measures, devoid of Logos.

The incarnation of the Logos becomes an event that human reason is increasingly unable to penetrate, precisely at a time in which thought draws the force of determination from the Logos for physical investigation. This force, today, is the only unknown of the thinking process. Therefore, the thinking process deprives itself of reality at the threshold of the sensory (realm) and legitimately finds this threshold insurmountable.

The unknown force of the determination is the living part of the thinking process. It does not lie outside this process, but within it. Being unaware of it renders thought inert at the threshold of the sensory. Present-day culture is evidence of the inability to penetrate the sensory, just as the Tradition, formally revived, is evidence of the soul's powerlessness to find the Logos, or the suprasensory. Both ignore the powers of thought bound to cerebralism, for which the whole soul succumbs to the sensory.

The inability to penetrate the sensory (realm) passes over into an unconscious idolatry of the physical world. But, by the same token, the revivification of the cadaver of the Tradition becomes the idolatry of a comparative series of symbols, myths and names, to which the original content cannot be restored, because of the inability to grasp the original force that expresses itself in the sensory (realm), since reflected thought is not overcome and since the spiritual practice of thinking is disavowed.

Without overcoming the cerebral mediation that renders thought reflected, an elevation to the real content of alchemy, of the Grail, is impossible. Access to the Logos, to the New Mysteries is barred. Nominalist esotericism arouses forces, which, unaware of their source, impede liberation. By not overcoming the cerebral limit, they cannot overcome the sphere of mediumship. One becomes strong and full of mystical and magical inspiration, but remains the laughing stock of instincts and of passions. The presumed esoteric edifice is erected on the clay foundations of feeling, incapable of escaping the subjective limit, because it is incapable of overcoming the cerebral mental sphere.

Nevertheless, we have been able to consider how overcoming duality in the intuitive pre-dialectical moment, as a power of identity and synthesis of the "I"—itself one with the Logos—rendered mathematical–physical thought possible. This thought unconsciously draws on the Logos, but on the plane of reflected freedom, it opposes the Logos. It rejects it in accordance with a power of opposition that it has never possessed with respect to the Divine. This prepares the worsening of the present-day human crisis, which is the general request of human consciousness to the Logos, certainly not by means of physicists, or mathematicians, or technologists, but by means of those "in charge" of the spiritual.

The germ of overcoming duality is the soul's transcendent reality. The Logos that becomes flesh is the image of an event that can be initially experienced by us, as spiritual practitioners, in the pre-dialectical synthesis of thought, which is not thought but the current of life. In such a synthesis, we begin to experience the resurrection of what is dead within us, what continuously dies—namely, reflected thought, the negation of light. We rediscover the light. Resurrection is the life of what *has overcome the world*, insofar as it has overcome duality within itself. It is the power of synthesis of the Divine with the human being, for which the original element, capable of expressing itself as the power of individuality, is restored to the human being.

In the living moment of thinking, the "I" begins to experience the Light of the World, which has overcome the separation. It is a power that demands to be identified—not thought, not represented, and not intuited but rather *perceived*. This is the act of freedom—namely, the ultimate sense of dialectical freedom, which begins as opposition to the principle of the light, from which it arises.

The Divine becomes human; the human reconnects with the Divine, within Christ. Whoever treads the path of initiation—whoever recognizes or fails to recognize the Christ—knows, at a given moment on the path, that there is no initiation without such a teacher. It is not the recognition of the name that matters, but the recognition of the force. The spiritual practitioner must overcome the interminable series of esoteric mirages to realize that initiation has only one source, the Christ—certainly not the mystical, or gnostic, Christ or the Christ limited to a religion but, rather, the cosmic Christ, the metaphysical principle of absolute individuality and freedom.

True *esotericism* provides the disciple with the means to recognize the force present in the "I" that overcomes the soul's subjection to corporality—the subjection for which the human coincides with the human–animal and subjects the heart's original forces to the cerebral organ. True esotericism is what enables the disciple to free, within the head, the heart's original forces and to overcome, by means of this path, the human–animal subjection, from which arises the dual vision of the world.

The Logos—overcomer of duality—is that with which the "I," within itself, is one. From this, its source, the "I" can draw the inexhaustible force, the primordial force, or that for which it is radically an "I" that overcomes the human–animal. The secret of the New Mysteries is the path of the greatest negation and the greatest affirmation of the "I."

Monism—the ideal of all the systems of oriental wisdom, from the Brahmanas to Vedanta, to Buddhism, to Taoism, to Zen, as well as of all the paths of Islamic and Christian gnosis, namely the ideal of metaphysical universality, the resolver of duality—has never effectively overcome the intractability of the mental sphere. It really has nothing to do with the mental sphere or the nonmental sphere. In the course of the spirit's history, each spiritual practitioner sure of having overcome the mental plane, has always, in effect, merely overcome the dialectical barrier, not the mental sphere. Each of them was able to overcome the mental only on the condition of being freed of the human and of ascending to ecstasy, leaving the human at the mercy of animal corporality and leaving the problems of duality, error, sickness, and death unresolved.

Only the original force itself can say "I am the Light of the World" with regard to itself, since, as the life of the light, it has incarnated at the level of earthliness, or of animal corporality. It can recapture the human bound to earthliness, overcome duality, and conquer error, sickness and death. Duality is overcome there, where the incarnation of the Divine in the human is realized. Error and sickness are overcome by the manifestation of the powers of truth and healing born by the principle that realizes such an incarnation. Only the original force itself, resolving, within itself, the limit of earthliness in the incarnation, can overcome duality and thus defeat death. The "I" is the "I" because it has this original force within it. It has only one task—to be the "I" that it is, to be according to the Logos, not according to the soul's subjection to corporality, in whose animal element—pure, in itself despite the inferior—it is corrupted. Nature truly becomes sinful within the human being.

The ideal of initiations and of traditions, the transcendence of the human and the human realization of the Divine, the millenary yearning of the initiates, saints, and spiritual practitioners, is realized for the first time as a concrete process in the Earth's *"invisible"* (realm), by way of the visible ritual of Christ. But it is not the revelation that can give an account of the transcendent content of such an action to the modern human being, because the organ capable of perceiving the revelation in the soul today does not exist, or rather, has yet to be reconstituted. It underwent a gradual atrophy, little by little, so that the inner human being would go identifying ever more with physical corporality. The inner human being truly succumbed to the swooning of the "I." The "I" died down as a spiritual principle and, simultaneously, the human began to have rational and philosophical, or even cerebral knowledge of it, as well as a concrete experience of it only as a physical *ego*.

In fact, the primordial force of the "I" became intimately reawakened within the soul by the Impulse of the Logos—the resolver of the animal–human, since it is the vanquisher of death. It was the germ of the initiatory restitution of the principle of the "I." However, this restitution requires, within the soul, the *free act* of the human being to be realized. The "I" has the task of being the "I" that it is, independent of the soul, so that the soul can discover its cosmic nature, independent of the human–animal imprint.

The impulse of the Logos is what the "I" was primordially. Though remaining metaphysically immutable, the "I" had fallen humanly into corporeal unconsciousness. At this level, it secretly recovered the power of movement of its own original essence. Thanks to the identity with the inner force of the Logos, it sought the direct path within the soul through the determination of thought in the sensory realm, it itself bearing the intuition of its own being within thought—all this according to a process, donated but not won, yet winnable by the free human being, who can, however, be free only within the Earth's sphere of darkness.

This thought, having within its nucleus the original power of the revelation, as we said, moved in an unknown and nevertheless intuitively conscious way, the initial investigators of the sensory realm—Copernicus, Galileo, Newton, and so on.

The current of life in which the identity with the Divine could initially incarnate (to the extent that it was donated) was *feeling*. But, so that this identity could become a human conquest, or germinal, divine magic within the human being—namely, itself the *individual* incarnation of the Logos—it had to arise as the volitional determination of the "I" within the soul. It had to be a creative ideal, the germ of *thinking* capable of penetrating matter—the germ of conscious responsibility, which gave humanity the possibility of choosing freely between Essence–Logos and what opposes it on Earth.

Only where we have the capacity to negate the Logos, within the sphere of earthly necessity, can we freely choose the path of the Logos. For the human being of the new times, an unfree choice of the Logos is inconceivable. The current of free will is the bearer of the authentic force, or of the force of the "I" that can operate with absolute independence from earthly, human–animal necessity.

Whoever seeks the Logos along the paths of the Tradition, is not aware of essentially following a path of feeling rather than one of consciousness. Within thinking, as a rational activity, we rightly feel that we are unable to find the Logos. Therefore, we seek it by means of traditional consciousness, but we fail to notice that the intuitive element, to which we appeal for such research, no longer lies within feeling, but at the source of the thinking by means of which we think.

Christian mystics and saints had the mission of incarnating the human–divine synthesis of the Logos within feeling, at a time when the organ of self-consciousness had yet to be formed. They were able to incarnate it within the impulse of devotion, not within the will correlated to thought—as should have begun occurring in the Galilean type of investigator—and thus on condition that thought did not presume to comprehend the Logos. This was a wise attitude, because, in effect, thought that is merely human cannot comprehend the Logos.

The current task of thinking, nonetheless, is not to comprehend or to intuit the Logos—a rhetorical undertaking, conceivable only on the basis of a limited understanding of the dialectical limit of thought. The task of thinking is to incarnate the element of life that lies within it and from which it alienates itself to become dialectical—an element of suprasensory life from which it moves and without which it would not be, even when it takes on the error. The task of thinking is to realize its own intuitive nucleus, in which the Logos is present as an original force. Thought must arise again as magical thinking.

The connection with the Logos today cannot be the work of feeling, whose function has lapsed into a passive "resonating" based on subjective contents, within the ambit of reflected consciousness. The feeling of the Divine must rise again from a state of death. It is, more than ever, the force of the Work, but, as such, it needs to be reawakened. At one time, the *mystes* or the saint could, within feeling, abandon him or herself to the realm of the Logos, not through an act of will, but through a radical renunciation of the individual element of the will. What he or she carried out that was prodigious was an act of the Logos *by means of* him or herself. Today, the experience of the Logos appeals only to the will's individual element. But this arrives at feeling, passing by way of thought. In the ascetics of the Tradition, sentiment was certainly not the anemic and psychic feeling of modern human beings, but the original force of super-individual and cosmic feeling, surviving exceptionally. In them, such feeling operated as a suprasensory vehicle, in wait for the era of individual will and of freedom, that is, the era in which the Logos can have a center of force in self-consciousness and be nourishment for the "I." Within consciousness itself, spiritual practitioners can experience the original virtue of the thinking mediation, or total immediacy. They can contemplate the will's initial individual element as descending from the Logos.

This discourse is neither theological nor mystical, let alone philosophical. Rather, it is exclusively practical. True realism is to discover that we do not lack the "I" but, rather, the soul. This means that we are missing the soul's relationship to the "I." With the soul resounding exclusively throughout the sensory (realm), only thought can be the vehicle of the "I," or of the spirit, within the soul. But thought can overcome the reflected state, as subjection to the sensory, since it has at its disposal the force acquired within the sensory.

The soul that today, in its normal condition, tends to open up to the spiritual, by methods that ignore the mediation of thought, cannot help but open up to lower forms of power and pleasure, which increasingly bind the soul, or even the reflected "I," to corporality, thereby strengthening the *ego*. Saints and mystics could still open their souls to the Logos, within the vehicle of feeling, at a time which can be said to be preparatory with respect to modern times. The Logos had yet to have, as an immediate vehicle within consciousness, thought capable of expressing (in the *giving of itself* to the sensory realm) the power of identity of the "I." In reality, thought's giving of itself to the sensory is the consciousness soul's initial movement of will and love, which the consciousness soul has yet to know.

The life of ancient feeling is exhausted. Its passage toward the Logos closed itself within the soul the moment thinking became connected to the sensory, individualizing itself through the mathematical–physical determination of quantity. The sheer resonating of physical alterity within the soul has paralyzed the mediation of feeling. The devout and mystical feeling of modern human beings is a parody with respect to that of which the ancient human being was capable. As an impulse of identity with the sensory (realm), the ancient power of feeling, the giving of itself, has moved within thinking—from whose obtuse consciousness materialism springs forth. The force of self-giving must become conscious to thinking, so that it can reawaken feeling and overcome materialism.

The source of the ancient faith has dried up and weak subjective feeling is left in its place, capable of resonating only by way of the values of physical life. Unable to resound according to the Logos, feeling yearns for communion with this Logos, by way of profound nostalgia, but unknowingly, therefore, without hope and without any other means of escape but pain.

The path of living thinking is ultimately the *conscious* discovery of the force of the ancient *faith*. Such a force returns as the organ of immanent certainty. The Solar Initiate of the new times has the highest suprasensory vision and traces its path, so that disciples can follow this path with the "I" in the "imaging" that has been freed and experience their own cosmic history. Whoever fails to understand this process and thinks of the non-anthropomorphic descriptions of the events of suprasensory experience, like a brilliant spiritual daydreaming, still lacks the forces to grasp the sense of the will born of self-consciousness at the sensory level.

The will inherent in self-consciousness is the germ of a new human–cosmic force. It is born within the concept, or within the idea, or within freed imagining. The magical path of the new times is possible only to those who understand how modern human beings have the possibility to overcome matter by way of the concept. The concept is, within itself, an image–synthesis. The "I" that encounters such an image–synthesis moves in something that has, within itself, the force of being carried out in living reality. The "I" discovers, in a conscious state, the force of the ancient faith within the inner life of the concept.

The ancient faith and the mediation of super-individual feeling were once possible, thanks to an action of the Logos within the soul, which demanded the exclusion of rational consciousness, of egoic initiative, of thinking autonomy. It was a gift of the Logos, rather than the conquest of the "I." It was not the victory of individual willing over the *ego*. The ascetic's *ego* was not ruled by the individual "I" but, rather, by the force of the higher "I," which transcended it and demanded that it abandon earthly things and individual will to be operative in it.

The Logos could operate provided that the "I" remained silent. It was not the "I" that determined itself, but the Logos that became determination within the "I"—a gift that human beings could not yet realize as substantiality, because it could be gathered by them only on condition of excluding the initiative of the "I," as well as consciousness of the "I" itself.

The presence of the Logos within the soul is realized by means of the free "I." This freedom, which is the possibility for the greatest autonomy within the sensory achieved at the sensory level, is simultaneously the possibility for the greatest identity with the Logos. Real freedom is equivalent to the *greatest dependence* on the Logos. The more the "I" realizes its free being, the more it is identical to the Logos. Devotion to the Logos is the ultimate sense of human freedom and, at the same time, the secret of the conscious resurrection of the ancient faith.

The *direct* path of the Logos within the soul is that of waking consciousness. Normally, within feeling, we realize a dream consciousness; we are not awake. We are awake within thinking, that is, within the soul's lowest activity, because it is the most bound to the sensory but, simultaneously, the only one of which we can determine, by means of a lucid waking state, the dissolution from the sensory. The spiritual or pre-dialectical part of thinking is also immersed in the sleeping state, but we can operate indirectly by means of it with correct waking thought. We have the capacity to ascend to it by realizing its inner force at the lucid waking level through concentration and meditation. In that sense, the spiritual practice of thinking is the path to the Logos. The bond of consciousness to the sensory (realm) on account of thought—if not overcome by thought itself—renders consciousness deaf to any resonance of the Logos, of which only the empty name remains, filled with mystic sentimentalism.

Thinking's secret power of life is the Logos, but it is also feeling's power of life, as well as that of the will. Within thinking, however, the presence of the Logos is immediate. Disciples can directly encounter such a presence through the spiritual practice of thinking. They can experience the kindling of thought in the astral, where the "I" surfaces. Thinking's power of identity with the sensory, the dedication of thinking to the sensory, responsible for the birth of natural science, is, in itself, the power of life of the Logos.

The aim of concentration is to awaken, within thinking, the inner power of life immersed within the sleep of supra-consciousness. Thanks to this liberation, feeling is revived according to its source of life and loses the possibility of binding the soul to the everyday misery of personal pleasure and pain, of attraction and repulsion. Feelings become the life sustenance of the soul, insofar as they are able to flow within the *heart*, which gathers them and sends them back purified, radiating anew into the world.

By means of ordinary feeling, we are ruled by a cosmic entity that tends to furnish us with experiences of the spirit that satisfy our *ego*. It also furnishes us with vital forces—of ephemeral consistency—provided that we are not free, but depend on it. This feeling, insofar as it is conditioned by thinking bound to the senses, because of a cerebral path, cannot flow toward the heart. In order for this to happen, we need the current of the will as a vehicle. We cannot, however, recover such a current, except by taking it away from the luciferic entity's control. The current of the will demands the liberation of thinking, or the spiritual practice of concentration in the seat of the soul where waking consciousness lights up. Disciples can access the New Mysteries if they are able to perceive the point at which the astral body lights up from the flaming splendor of the "I" when the dynamic moment of thinking is firmly willed.

An essential technique to reawaken the feeling of the Divine by means of thought is as follows. When we are aware of mastering the discipline of concentration, we can train ourselves to behold the rising up of a thought and to grasp it before it assumes a dialectical form. We devote ourselves to following its movement, as it thereby follows its own course, by not becoming reflected. If we are careful, we see this movement connect with the heart. A further experience consists in holding to the level of this passage of nonreflected thought from the head to the heart—a level that becomes lost if we are seized by the sensation of blessedness that legitimately emanates from the heart, not as a sensory movement but, rather, as one that is suprasensory and, nonetheless, destined to expire in the body if immediately felt. Mystical prevention is the impediment—namely, not beholding the priority of the thinking-force.

The genuine experience begins when the perception of the non-dialectical thinking that flows toward the heart enables us to perceive the forming of thought immediately connected to it and this, too, is gathered before the dialectical form and is seen setting off toward the heart. And we know that it connects with the heart, although we are attentive to the immediately succeeding thought, by means of which the operation is repeated, and so forth—like receiving a supra-mental whole that occurs rhythmically, the universal perceptible, thanks to the forces developed in physical "existing," which indeed requires thought capable of being immersed into the physical but, simultaneously, being redeemed in accordance with the source of the heart.

This is the preliminary path, by means of which the current of thinking receives the living element, which, insofar as it is living, is in itself, pre-dialectically connected with the current of the heart. It is the path that readies the experience of the Christ within thinking. The flowing of thought becomes the flowing of the Christ-force, insofar as each thought realizes its own conversion in arising. Such flowing cannot remain pure super-mental light. It must enter the human mental (sphere), where it normally deteriorates as dialectical thought. The conversion of this is precisely the conscious kindling of its pure, pre-dialectical moment.

At this point, a secret ritual of thought is grasped, which introduces the New Mysteries and opens up the passage to the regenerating current of the Earth. The preparation for such a ritual is the work of disciples, but its form and its content remain unknown to them until the spiritual world allows them to perceive it. Investigators, still within individual limits, are unable to gauge their own maturity to this end.

Above all, we must cognize the flowing of thought as a pure continuous relation—unbound to anything and nevertheless metaphysically present as the essential connection of everything—as the inner content of every sensory perception, and as the pure concept. Such flowing is normally unknown except in its lower form of dialectical continuity, which proceeds according to the determination of thought by way of the sensory and is, therefore, experienced as a connection conditioned by the corporeal support and by the physical multiplicity.

The flowing responds to the superhuman nature of thought. Its substance is a transcendent golden light that contains the resurrected force of feeling. In order for its flow to become human, it is not enough that a passage be open to it. Any mental movement toward it opposes it. Any thought that thinks it, rejects it. Thought must operate at a level where it is not adverse to the Logos. This level is realized by the force that thought develops as a *donation* of itself to the sensory. The level of its fall is also that of its rediscovery, because it is that of its freedom. Such a level should be known. Only within that level can the thinking that bears the greatest power of will, be freed. Such is the sense of the spiritual practice of thinking indicated by us.

What has become human as the incarnated Logos can be seen surfacing as an intuitive germ of the thinking that manifests by way of the sensory (realm). This germ can be recognized as the point of confluence between the celestial intelligence and human thinking. It can be realized by the thinking that gives itself to the sensory, without fear of losing itself. It was naturally possessed in its purity by the first Western investigators of the sensory (realm). Now, it must be rediscovered in such purity. To those investigators, it was never conscious. The spiritual practice of new investigators consists in realizing it in a conscious state. It is the higher path of the "I."

We have seen how dialectical thinking opposes its own intuitive source, for which it abstractly uses concepts that nevertheless rise up from the intuitive moment. Ordinarily, there is nothing but a discursive relation between these concepts. There is no internal relation. Therefore, the flowing of thought as an organic continuity is not possible. And so, the correlation of love—which is the correlation of the "I"—is impossible for the soul. This results from being unaware of the moment of thinking's donation to the sensory, which is the moment of the Divine's flow into the human astral—the point in which the "I" is born within thinking.

Spiritual practice must enable the researcher to experience the *pure concept*, to the point of being able to detect its inner power of connection with every other concept, according to the original impulse of the thinking that occurs by way of the sensory. Such a connection must be called upon until it occurs through its own power, according to its transcendent manifesting.

This manifesting is the light of life flowing into the soul, within the formative moment of the concept. The light of life is the same in each and every concept. For this reason, concentration on any object leads to it, thanks to the identification of its substantial nucleus. Experiencing the flow of the pure series of thoughts gives rise to the possibility of encountering sensory forms by means of their inner content. The Logos is restored to the world that appears dual, because it is devoid of it.

Deprivation is the condition of the "I" divorced from the Logos. Such deprivation lies at the origin of the world's state of material necessity, namely of its being the permanent solidification of the spiritual *past*, which is the past of the entire being, including what is the psychophysiological support of the spirit within us. Here, we are at the continuous mercy of desire, of error, and of sickness. We human beings, who are such to the extent that we identify with the *completed* structures of our own animic–physical beings, oppose the Superhuman. Obstructors operate in categories in which the human past is expressed in minerality, in the psyche, and in cerebralism.

Within pure thinking flows the ever-new element of the spirit, independent of the past and, therefore, of *karma*. Within this flow, the investigator has the possibility of a secret ritual of thinking, where the living content of the Advent of Christ is realized, which is the ultimate sense of thinking—our correlation with the Divine, the resurrection of spiritual feeling, by means of which the Divine enters the human being.

9

MANIFESTATION OF THE LIGHT: THE IDEA

We cease to receive the gift of the Logos within the sphere of the soul that corresponds to the sleep or dream state. The feeling of the Divine must become the experience of the "I." We human beings who are awake, who are autonomous—to the extent that we are independent of the ancient suprasensory connection—possess the requirements to embrace our own inner principle, the secret lymph of waking life. We can willfully restore the connection with the suprasensory, the direct connection. But we must work from the stage in which we become self-conscious. We cannot pass over this step (which is the lowest) in which we realize the initial dimension of autonomy. Actually, no one can pass over it. Passing over it can only be the illusion of whoever cultivates the cushy force, or the simple calm, or the effortless devotion.

The spiritual continues to be operative within the inner soul, but the connection can no longer be the ancient one. Something has changed within the depths, of which we have yet to be cognizant. We can reach such depths if we do not abandon the thread of consciousness by means of which we begin to achieve self-knowledge. This thread can lead us far if we follow it. But we can follow it only if we recognize it. It is the first subtle trickle of a torrent that will become impetuous, containing the force of the concatenation of worlds. The true *magical path* does not allow itself to be possessed unless one is on the thread of clear consciousness, of its limitless self-surrender to the Logos, of the soul's volitional rigor with itself in relation to one's neighbor—absolutely overcoming every *pólemos* in spite of differences, for which the magical path is the path of fraternal harmony, the human sense of the hierarchy of forces that discover their own center.

The *willed idea*, from the center of its own "forming," connects the "I" with the Logos, because for it the current of thinking passes over into the current of the will. The idea, willed from the depths of its own form, frees feeling from the subjective prison and allows it to reconnect with the heart. The harmony of the three forces, thinking, feeling and willing, is the threshold to the New Mysteries.

The idea not penetrated becomes a demand of the exhausted connection, despite the correct intention—a regressive impulse. Nonetheless, if the correct intention possesses the corresponding impulse of the will, it cannot but realize its own idea-force over time. The traditional connection is to be cognized, but it must not condition the concrete continuity as perpetuity, independent of the past forms grasped by means of present dialectical thinking.

Turning to the forms of the Tradition, like to the actual contents of the spirit, runs the risk of arresting the journey, as much as a passive adherence to the world of quantity. Denial of the modern world does not, therefore, outweigh the level of its acceptance as a value. Spiritual Science speaks of two obstructors operating in the subtle body of the human being—one from the suprasensory (realm), the other from the sensory (realm)—Lucifer and Ahriman. When human beings believe they combat one of the two aspects of evil, they naïvely believe that its opposite is good. Meanwhile, it is the other aspect of the same evil.

It is always the evil of duality that waits to be overcome by human beings who bear the cause within them, within fallen thought. However, they also bear the possibility of the resolving synthesis. The Logos that has become flesh is present within the soul as the germinal power of thought, because it is the virtue of the original synthesis, operating as the concept's suprasensory moment, which occurs by way of perceptible objectivity.

The synthesis is continuously splintered into dialectical thinking, at the level of sensory perception, whose content, unpenetrated, constitutes the alterity and gives rise to matter as an objective substantiality, with an "essence" of its own; indeed, it is simply thought, but without one being aware of thinking it, thanks to reflected thought, devoid of the original synthesis. The task that awaits us is to ascetically realize this power of determination in thinking.

The presence of the Logos is latent in every thought that we think. We have the principle of freedom within our grasp. We continuously use it, but we squander its power, unknowingly. In sensory perception, we continuously have its magical immediacy, but it is so inherent in the sensory datum that we identify this principle with the datum and lose it within crude sensation.

In regards to the *Philosopher's Stone*, one of the first communications on its existence, toward the end of the eighteenth century, alludes to its *materia prima* (raw material) as something that everyone has available to them daily. This *materia prima* is actually the original life element of perception and of thought, which therefore flows unconsciously even within the breath. Today, whoever points out a different path toward the Philosopher's Stone deceives the spiritual seeker, even if it is true that these (seekers) need such a deception to overcome a specific trial of the *preparation*.

Within sensory perception lies the secret of thought's initial life. It arises already integrated by the Logos. The investigator who chances upon the subtle life of sensory perception has the initial life of the Logos in non-dialectical thinking.

The sensory impression must not be explained (as psychophysiology naïvely presumes) by the world of vibrations behind it—which, insofar as they are themselves sensorial impressions, consequently raise the issue of their perception—but, rather, by means of its own manifesting. This manifesting is to be contemplated; it is not to be dialecticized. But, to this end, it demands that distinction from it of the "I" which leads to the contemplative experience of thought—the *manifesting* of thought. Normally, consciousness is one with perception, just as it is with thought. The "I" is not distinguished from them. The distinction is the birth of the "I," which is truly one with that from which it can distinguish itself, not with that from which it does not know how to distinguish itself. The "I" that notices the manifesting of thought, truly possesses thought, and within thought it grasps the will. From thought's rediscovered correlation with the will, there springs the liberated life of feeling—the true *bhakti*.

Sensory reality exists, but it effectively occurs at the scene of consciousness, as a continuous inner experience, whose wealth of life escapes ordinary waking consciousness, which is arrested at sensation and at representation, where the "I" is the subject involved. It is not the real subject. Moreover, the experience of the suprasensory current escapes, since waking consciousness would be overwhelmed by its power of life, if it could allow this power to burst in on it, without adequate forces of identification. The discipline of concentration and pure observation, or pure perception, prepares consciousness to open up to its own power of life, or Logos. In reality, it is the birth of the "I." The "I" begins to distinguish itself from the datum that gives itself to it not only as a sensory object, but also as thought—the inner content of the object. By distinguishing itself, the "I" finally rules the current of the will, over which it has no power so long as it is engaged in thoughts.

The "I" that experiences not only the manifesting of the object, but also the manifesting of the thought that integrates it—not as dialectical thought, but as an inner content—cooperates in a cosmic process taking place, in that it brings to fulfillment, the integration of the sensory datum, already begun within perception. The Logos is present in ordinary perception, because it is present to perception in pure immediate, pre-dialectical, inner thinking, as the vehicle of consciousness.

The "I" that experiences the manifesting of thought, as well as the manifesting of perception, begins to live within a new current of the will. It experiences the flowing of thought as a flowing of the will. It can also call this current *Kundalini*, but it is truly the Logos, the force of profound feeling, or of celestial love, which continuously surfaces and is extinguished as the determination of everyday thought.

The determination of thought becomes the deception of all existing if it is not transformed into the will's determination by means of the spiritual practice that thought demands according to the very process of its manifesting. It has manifested precisely because of this, to grasp the force of its own determination, or its own current of life. This current flows uninterrupted. However, rejected by the consciousness soul, it deviates toward its multifaceted alienation in instincts and passions.

Through discipline, we, as spiritual practitioners, discover that, for us, thought is a *datum*, just like any other datum of the world, outer or inner. It is, however, the datum of immediate consciousness. We experience the manifesting of thought as an initial manifesting of the suprasensory realm. Above all, we discover that thought does not belong to us. It is not our production. It is given to us, just as the sensory world is given to us on the physical plane. In essence, we normally use thinking to feel ourselves egoistically, since we are still incapable of living within the "I," which alone can disregard thought.

Experiencing thought as something external, or objective, reveals to us, as spiritual practitioners, the secret of liberation, primarily because it restores to thought its function regarding living ideas—then finally, to be and to feel ourselves be, because we do not need to think; we *witness* our own thoughts. By means of such an experience, in moments of meditation and of contemplation, the original *dynamis* of thinking is revealed to us as a cosmic current of life that normally descending into us, alienates itself and becomes lifeless, insofar as we unconsciously identify with it so as to be conscious of ourselves, to feel ourselves be, to know our own nature. Normally, we identify with our own thinking and thereby de-realize it. In strengthening thought, we, as spiritual practitioners, essentially set into motion the "I," or the principle that, in itself, does not require thinking to be connected to the world.

The cosmic current of thinking, descending into the mental sphere, alienates itself as dialectical thinking; but precisely in the mental sphere, we, as spiritual practitioners, by overcoming the dialectical limit, separate thought from ourselves and contemplate it until beholding its manifesting. It is the contemplation of this manifesting that frees us from the *desire of thinking* and frees thought from the egoistic imprint with which we continuously alter it out of dialectical necessity. To experience pure thinking means to perceive the living element of concepts and of ideas as an objective force, freed from the need to express egoic–sentient nature. In reality, we normally de-realize thought by means of the desire inclined to assert its own sentient necessity. Therefore, we obtusely identify with thought. We believe it to be our own. We attach ourselves to it. We cannot do without it. We are possessed by it. Instead, animal nature possesses us through our thinking. When such a situation is given a dialectical–logical form, the result is present-day culture with its ideologies of quantity, as well as the esotericism that ignores the path of the Logos.

The initial achievement of spiritual practice is the liberation of thought from the desire of the thinking expression of the lower astral. The desire of thought, attachment to thought, identifying with thought, and continuously letting oneself be transported by thought are essentially the enslavement of thinking to the sentient, or astral, body's desire for sensations. The ahrimanic inversion of the function of thought generates the human being's connection with the human–animal.

In reality, thought does not normally serve the spirit but rather its physical alienation. The exercise of concentration restores thought to the "I." It frees thought from *sentient tenacity*. If such liberation overcomes the psychic limit, thought manifests as a force in itself, independent of the astral body—a force continuously bestowed by the suprasensory. This is like saying that the "I" is dis-identified from the astral body. It can now operate on the astral. The astral can be pacified. It begins to resonate according to the *harmony* of the original structure, owing to the fact that its subjection to physical nature is deprived of the thinking expression.

Those of us who are able to realize thinking as a fact are free, because, by not depending on thoughts, our "I" is not enveloped by the astral body; instead, it controls it. Thinking reaches us from the spiritual world and becomes for us its fabric of revelation and, simultaneously, a current of life and of love, which reunites, within itself, the suprasensory nature of light and of fire. In this current, the "I" has the support and image of its own gift. The spiritual practitioner can now know that the *essence* of such a gift is the Logos. He or she can experience the cosmic Christ.

From the point of view of initiation, it is crucial that we recognize within the suprasensory forces of living nature, the spiritual currents controlled by the needs of the manifestation at the sentient, vital, and physical levels. All of nature appears to us as the symbol of the Divine's *transcendent presence*, the sign of the *past* presence, the imprint, in which the creative moment of the forms is no longer in effect. The suprasensory in such forms is no longer present, except as a mechanical *repetition,* or as an echo. Regarding the Logos, which is the origin of such forms, we have the possibility of resurrection, since we are free at the heart of the earthliness that is in need. We have the possibility of resurrection in the original moment of thinking that—by being familiar with the freeing from sensory necessity—discovers its own cosmic movement. We retrace the thinking of the Fall, insofar as we objectively grasp the movement of thinking that is immediate to us.

As spiritual practitioners of the new times, we learn, as a task of initiation, to meet the forms of creation devoid of the Logos by means of the pure current of the "I." Cosmic thinking, which was in the beginning, can rise up within us insofar as the "I" realizes freedom at the level of the fall. It is the thinking that overcomes the animal nature of the human being—the thinking of the victorious re-ascension, or of the Resurrection. The "I" must encounter the perceptions of the world in the purest form, so that the Logos creator, resounding within the soul, can be restored as a germinal force of the future Earth.

Today, through the technique of liberating thought, we realize the *idea* as an idea-force insofar as we grasp the concept's original impulse of life, or that of the thinking which manifests by way of an object. Ancient ascetics knew thinking, but tapped into the force beyond it. They did not know the idea but rather the "universal," which was transcendent to them. In place of the idea, they had inspiration, as a power whose irresistibility and vastness are inconceivable to modern dialectical thought.

As modern spiritual practitioners, we can discover this irresistibility and vastness if thought's force of determination, experienced, leads us to the *perception* of the idea. We can recognize each existing entity as the petrification of an original idea. Petrified ideas or ideas confined to a mechanical movement necessitated by their archetypal being are forms of nature. We, however, bear within us the principle of the supernatural. We can relive, within our very selves, the original power of the idea, which preceded the petrification and the mechanization. The Hegelian view of nature is precise in this regard, but it does not go beyond the idea conditioned in its movement by the form necessary to nature. Regardless of how dynamic it is in its immanence, the idea does not overcome the dialectical limit. It does not reach the cosmic. The idea again becomes living only if it is recovered by the principle, independent of the human being, or independent of natural or dialectical necessity. Then, it again draws on life from its own center. But this can happen thanks to the fact that consciousness finds its own center of life, the Superhuman, within itself.

Freed thinking can retrace the idea's movement to the archetype, so that the idea can restore the power of life within the soul. It is revived from its center. At the level of mineral nature, there springs for us this element of freedom, or the very principle itself of which the creative idea, confined to the mechanism of nature, is deprived. We can overcome the dialectical moment of the idea by reviving within ourselves—thanks to the element of freedom—the cosmic movement that has become petrified or mechanized within the entity. This cosmic movement refers us to the principle, to the Logos, to the threshold of the New Mysteries, within the depths of the soul.

The secret of the idea is its "emerging" from its own center, from which it draws the power of life. Without this power of life, the idea could not be of value to consciousness. With the idea, consciousness finds itself before an entity endowed with automatic life, which contains the foundation, the source of its own being. The creative entities of the cosmos truly approach us by means of ideas.

We experience the idea, in that we encounter it at its source, until we feel it spring from our own interiority. Wherever we fail to encounter such a source, we know that we are before a content that needs *explanation*, but with this we are again cast into dialectics, or into rhetoric—namely, into the sphere of ideas devoid of life and, therefore, necessary to logically justify the human being.

The human is the human–animal that tends to enslave the idea to avoid the transmutation according to its own original impulse, which is the impulse of cosmic–human love. Human beings are bound to their own dialectics by the hidden terror of having to attain freedom from their own animal nature, that is, of having to overcome ideology, the doctrine that codifies their bondage to instincts. When we refer to the New Mysteries, to an initiatory path of the new times, we are alluding to something that goes beyond the spiritualism and Idealism characterized by an anthropomorphic limit, for which the idea is, certainly, the mystical or spiritualistic idea, but in itself is the expression of the human being, which is the human–animal. To free the human being from the human–animal is to open a human gateway to superhuman love.

The idea is a force that has, within it, its own *center*. Either we control it, or we are controlled by it. When we are controlled by it, the human–animal is expressed by means of it. The idea asks to be possessed by the inner principle of life that it bears within it. Investigators know that to penetrate such a principle one must will it. However, one can will it only by means of thought so rigorously intensified that it can bring about its own silence, allowing only pure will to flow.

Thought arrives at the idea by passing over into the will. Once we, as disciples, elevate ourselves to living thinking, we essentially experience the creative current of the idea. We arrive at its center. Such a center is the principle of life that we can penetrate, insofar as we experience it from our own inner center, from the "I." The "I" realizes within the depths of the idea its own being as a power of identity. It experiences within a center of life, initially outside it, the essence of objectivity, to the degree at which it realizes absolute subjectivity. In absolute subjectivity, it transcends its own temporary psychic formation, which is the human–animal *ego*.

By means of the idea, we experience an archetypal germ in which the perennial powers of creation are urgently needed. It is not the abstract idea of philosophers, but the idea full of life that we can come to behold, when the current of the will awakens within thought. Through the thinking possessed thanks to regular discipline and, therefore, vitally reintegrated, we encounter the idea, which we must initially let live according to the power of synthesis before penetrating. In this way we penetrate the will-current of creation.

In the presence of the living idea, we (as investigators) cease to think. Thought serves us only as a pure vehicle or a movement of life of the "I" that perceives the idea. Within the idea we encounter a *living being*, that is, an intelligence endowed with the power to act according to an extra-human order, even if it is active within the earthly (sphere) and within the human being. It is the superhuman that constitutes the real basis of the human being, but that we normally do not know, since we conceive the human only in relation to our own anthropomorphic mental picturing, bound to the nervous system. This mental picturing, closed within the psyche, is closed to the reality of the universe. It is the idea that expresses the human–animal. The impurity lies not in the animal category, but in that of the human–animal, where Nature, in itself chaste, becomes sinful.

The fact that the perception of the idea elevates from a human order to a cosmic order, or to a world in which the human being has a foundation, is guaranteed to us by the fact that the foundation of an idea is not produced by us, but comes toward us, to the extent that we control and *silence* thought. The idea is a living being endowed with its own foundation. The art of the spiritual practitioner is to arrive at such a foundation. Plato saw it within a sphere that transcends the human being. We, as modern spiritual practitioners, realize it (to be) immanent as the culmination of the act of consciousness. We reach the heart of the world's objectivity, realizing within the idea the radical power of subjectivity, the "I," the Logos. As knowing beings, we encounter the world's creative entities.

To arrive at the idea, we must go beyond thought; we must possess the concept. In the concept, we have the core model of the idea. The idea flows analytically in thoughts, as the essence of thinking, the essence that dialectical thinking does not possess, for which it lacks life and truth. It compensates this lack with impulses of the subjective psyche, erecting dialectical structures devoid of a relation with reality. For this reason, however, one can say that the "ideas-force"* enters modern dialectical thought, in contrast to the "ideas-force" foundation of human reality.

The spiritual practitioner must control the idea so as to be able to encounter its center. It is good, therefore, to understand that such control is not to impede the idea from manifesting, or from revealing its own central being. To set oneself up as a ruler in the presence of the idea, means to defeat the instinctive powers of thought that rise up from the psyche to prevent thought from encountering its own essence, and to this end they suggest dialectical constructs. They are powers of the human–animal whose task is to obstruct the liberating function of the "I," its main identity with the cosmic–human.

The fundamental preparatory task is to possess the concept of the object by means of concentration. Within the pure concept, spiritual practitioners free themselves from the bonds of the dialectical psyche. The pure concept becomes for them the vehicle toward the sphere of creative ideas—the archetypes of entities, of bodies, of soul faculties, which is to say, the sphere of forces to which they appeal in meditation, evoking ideas and syntheses of ideas—entities in perennial movement close to the soul, like tiny suns around the interior Sun of the Logos, which shines as the power of the gift of the "I."

The infinite plurality of the "ideas-force" is maintained continuously by the unifying power of the Logos. Therefore, the follower of the Path can engender the formative "ideas-force" of human destiny from the center of the "I." Whether our essential activity gives rise to a demonic production, or to an angelic or suprasensory production

---

*   Here, Scaligero's term *idee-forza* is translated as "ideas-force," rather than "force of ideas," since the latter suggests a force composed of ideas rather than what is intended—namely, ideas as an indivisible force.

of ideas, depends on the human being responsible. The angelic production is the connection with the New Mysteries, to which the soul tends as if toward the reintegration of its own original nature.

10

THE NEW MYSTERIES

Once the powers of thought, aroused, take action and steer disciples toward the Great Work, they, at a given moment, demand that these disciples extinguish thought itself. At first, thought is transformed into a capacity of vision by means of images. This vision is necessary to the disciples' orientation in the suprasensory realm. But only when they are able to overcome this vision, are they able to enter the objective suprasensory realm; only then are they worthy of the total consecration of themselves.

Once the inner mental picturing that echoes the sensory realm is transcended, physical space is overcome. The world that disciples can access is woven of time, but it borders, at each of its twists, the world in which time is transcended, surfacing at each point as *duration*, or the entities' etheric time. The physical–cosmic destiny of things no longer appears petrified. The history of entities is re-enlivened in the context already created. Wherever non-dialectical thought arises as light, life continuously reveals itself in the moment of creative perpetuity, independently of human–animal vision, for which the natural cosmos already made, and the past as a condition of time, matter.

One crosses the threshold of a temple and knows that one enters the seat of the New Mysteries. Gradually, one comes to know the sacrarium of the Sun, from which the center of the heart draws the force, or the life of the light, normally rejected by mental thought. This thought becomes humanly strong, to the degree in which it expresses the human–animal and is rational and dialectical, or to the extent that its force draws on the ability to oppose the inner force of the heart, the sacrarium of the Sun. Human aversion, hate and desire are woven out of such thought, which justifies them.

The path that leads to the seat of the New Mysteries is thought that ceases to draw its own force from opposition to the light's source. On the contrary, one connects with such a source. The true path toward initiation is the esoteric knowledge that teaches the conversion, or transmutation, of dialectical thought, the secret of passing from reflected thought to living thinking.

Once the opposition is arrested, there emerges the condition for an encounter with the masters who bestow initiation and open the passage to the temple of the New Mysteries, so that disciples can know the sense of the subsequent path and the trials that still await them. They must know their relation to the sacrarium of the Sun, so that the image of it can be their guide in the moments of life where the primary intent seems overcome by the intensity of everyday *maya*.

Disciples are correlated to the New Mysteries, even when they have yet to perceive them and, nevertheless, proceed according to a correct spiritual practice. They receive orientation from knowledge and, by way of freed thinking, become independent not only of the *maya* of sensory existence, but also of the *maya* of outdated spiritual techniques. They are, however, connected with the sacrarium of the Sun, with which the spiritual entities and human disciples ritually unite at the borders of the sensory world, for the task of reintegration.

What becomes clear at a given moment to the disciple regarding the Path is the importance of becoming worthy of participating in such a Ritual, to which he or she is always indirectly connected. The connection requires secrecy and silence, so that independence from the *maya* of earthly things and from those that are deceptively spiritual can become a guiding power. From the initial spiritual practice of thinking, the source of the heart suggests the suprasensory meaning of the path initiated by the Master of the New Times toward the solar sacrarium, the place of fidelity and grand seriousness, where human conflict and the earthly evaluation of things makes no sense. Without knowledge of such a path, initiation today is impossible.

Great Seriousness is to take seriously, above all other values, the center from which the content of human destiny and world destiny springs, as a consequence of the will (elaborated in the sensory sphere) converging in it. The pure life of willing moves toward such a center, which is its original center. It can move as the essence of thought, as the essence of everyday sacrifice and of knowledge, of the giving of itself and of conscious liberation. It is the pure current of the will in which flows the thinking that frees itself from the opposition to the light of life, near the center of the heart, the force of identity with the content of the solar sacrarium.

The pure current of willing is the one that, by virtue of the Logos, descends into the depths of minerality and, therein, grasps the power of darkness to transform it into a flame of its original impetus of life. Icy hate and the tenacity of aversion are the powers of nature at the mineral level, with which the soul identifies unconsciously. Uncontrolled by the current of willing, they ascend as rulers, generating desire and aversion.

Thanks to the connection of the "I" with its original mysteries and, therefore, (thanks) to the virtue of Resurrection, the current of willing transforms the darkness of matter into light, icy aversion into the warmth of love, thereby allowing the inner force of matter to rise up from the nature of the Earth to that of Water, from this to that of Air, from this to that of Fire. Here, the ordinary impetus of life that, descending into the sensory (realm) becomes desire and aversion, is transformed into the warmth of love.

They are pure powers of nature, those that, not ruled by the current of the will, ascend within the soul as the powers of alteration, becoming desire and fear, anger and aversion, generating sickness and the necessity of death. The spiritual practice of thinking, as the concrete spiritual practice of the will, leads to the overcoming and the ruling of such powers, whose real purpose is to then become helpers. They are redeemed by the word *resurrector,* which can be pronounced by those who, knowing the path opened up by the Master of the New Times, discover the Logos within themselves. The current of willing is the current of the resurrection, which asserts, over the forces of darkness that generate desire, hatred and death, the power that defeats death and generates—as a flame of life—love, the conqueror of death. Therefore, the spiritual practice of this willing leads to the New Mysteries. But it is the spiritual practice of devotion, born as the spiritual practice of thinking. The path that, moving from thought, discovers the light and the original warmth of life can lead to the New Mysteries, because it is the path of the Grail.

The path of the Grail is one of reintegration, secretly yearned for by every human being in relation to an archetype inconceivable to reflected thought, even when such thought moves with spiritual intent. It is the discovery of what was lost, yet not annihilated, not destroyed, but rather immersed in sleep and in forgetfulness. The dream that springs from such sleep has become so intense that it appears real, and death becomes necessary so that awaking from it can occur. The path of the Grail is the awaking of life within the circle of the being that exists terrestrially, within the circle ruled by death.

Access to the kingdom of the Grail presupposes the knowledge of the New Mysteries, that is, the knowledge of the secret for which the current of the will, freed within thinking, draws directly from the Spirits of Will that move worlds. It is the current of the will, which has existed since the beginning of creation, and whose original moment we can restore as the redeeming principle of nature. In fact, within nature, this will operates estranged from its own principle. As human beings, we can be its liberator, if we implement the will that transforms icy minerality into the warmth of life and the current of hatred into the flame of "non-burning" love, continuously lighting itself up by consuming the earthly evil, the necessity of death.

It is the current of the will to which, as we have seen, the spiritual practice of thinking, by becoming the spiritual practice of the consecration of itself, confers the power of descending into the depths of the bodily structure, so as to connect dynamically with the will that has become the power of matter, or so as to discover and reawaken its own radical being within the darkness. This reconnection is liberating according to the Logos, because it is a sinking of devotion and of courage more powerful than the annihilation caused, at the sensory level, by desire. It is self-devotion that is willed, which descends in a redemptive way, there, where self-devotion is normally only a movement of desire, or the subjection of the soul's more elevated forces. Self-devotion, willed limitlessly, is, in fact, the consecration.

Eden is truly enclosed within the soul, a prisoner in depth of the usurpers of its light of life. The powers of desire feed on the alteration of this light of life, which is possible through swooning and the lack of knowledge of the soul. In those depths, only the forces of the *only begotten Son of the Father* are able to descend as liberators. They are the forces of the higher "I," which the new spiritual practice of thinking (that discovers the communion with the Logos) has the task of reawakening, because, by consuming desire, they alone lead to the New Mysteries. The solar sacrarium can again be found within the soul by whoever does not follow the illusory path of the Logos, but the real one, the path of living thinking, which is, in fact, the path of the Grail.

The solar sacrarium is the scene of the perennial resurrection of the higher "I," whereby the lower "I" carries out the sacrifice of its own force; and it can carry it out through love, because on the sensory plane it discovers the path of thinking as a path opposite to that of the fall. Through spiritual practice, thought is, in fact, sacrificed and redeemed, since, at the sensory level, it ceases to draw the force from its opposition to the light of the heart, to the solar sacrarium. It no longer receives certainty from the demon of the Earth.

Prior to such a sacrifice, each force is illusory, even if it is acquired by way of an ascetic path. But it is important that such a force exist. It is important that it expresses itself below as a force of the lower "I," so that the offer or the profound descent can be possible. In this sense, the path to the solar sacrarium is the path of the Grail.

The secret of the Grail is the ultimate aim of the spiritual practice of thinking, as a spiritual practice of consecration. It is this spiritual practice that awakens the current of the will capable of descending into the sphere of forces deeply engaged in maintaining the animal structure and of continuing its generation. It is a *descent* of redemption into the world of forces governed by desire and by *eros*, at the place where all human love is corrupted and extinguished. But it is the place where the power of a stronger love, endowed with the will that has discovered its solar source, can penetrate, thanks to the correct spiritual practice referred to as the spiritual practice of thinking. Actually, in the new times, the reintegration of the "I" into its suprasensory realm is its descent into the world of forces that organize corporeal existence and its physical continuity, as the continuity of the species. The descent, insofar as it is liberating, inevitably coincides with the resumption of the crucial experience of the forces of *eros* and, therefore, with the ultimate exigency of the mission of the human couple.

In my *Graal: Saggio sul mistero del sacro amore,** we were able to designate the experience of the Grail as a reconstitution of

---

*   "Grail: Essay on the mystery of sacred love" (not published in English).

the human couple's original accord, thanks to the resurrection (by way of a contemplative–operative path) of each soul's androgynous power, and thus according to the "solar" synthesis of such powers, individually resurrected. In accordance with the principle of not communicating teachings that cannot be answered according to an effectively completed experience, the series of images of a ritual of the contemplative–operative communion has been given, a communion possible to the human couple if it moves from the spiritual practice of the new times, which is the spiritual practice of the thinking–Logos, not contemplated by traditional methods.

The outline of the ritual springs from an experience of supermental forces, whose reawakening summons the current of the liberated will, based on a technique of thinking, continuously emphasized in our works as a path that, through the impulse of resurrection of the sacred, delineates for itself a precise methodological distinction. To believe that one finds, behind such an outline, the precedents of other teachings or analogies with some modern attempt of a *spagyric,* or hermetic–gnostic, schema cannot but be derived from a *lack of knowledge*—both the lack of knowledge of the hermetic–gnostic schema in question and of the content of the cited work.

The mentioned description of the path of sacred love responds to a volitional inner experience, independent of any esoteric–didactic presupposition, which proceeds only in conjunction with the logic of the liberated force, that opens the doorway to itself by means of inner triumphs and knowledge, that is, by means of the experimental connection with the cosmic powers of the soul. For us, the experience of reawakened powers of the "I," thanks to the correct spiritual practice, comes first, then the possible connection with the traditional symbols and morphologies, which is useful, but not strictly necessary.

The profound difference between the path indicated by us and the paths of formally traditional esotericism consists of the fact that this (esotericism), in current researchers (except in cases of exceptional personalities) identifies with the inner mental picturing that corresponds to the rationalistic–materialistic vision, by refusing the modern world and opposing that of other eras to it, based on knowledge, on symbolisms and on corresponding representations. However, it does not escape its anthropomorphic limit. It does not overcome the way of seeing that is humanly proper to it, because it ignores the dialectical limit, even if it is compensated with a substantially mystical *dynamis*. It merely knows what it bears within itself and that is true only in relation to consciousness as it humanly is. Meanwhile, the path of the Logos, or of the New Mysteries, consists in the experience of what we are *not* with respect to the actual state of consciousness, or what we are cosmically, in relation to our own corporeal structures—that is, in the volitional experience of what we genuinely are beyond the human, or "outside" the interiority limited to the nervous system, or to the most lifeless level of our corporality, or dialectical interiority instinctively led to include within itself the spiritual and the traditional.

The suprasensory experience fundamentally involves the discipline of thinking, since, within the modern human being, thinking is the only soul activity that moves in three worlds simultaneously— the physical, animic, and spiritual. When it moves below, it simultaneously moves above. In its lower course, thought is able to operate in a ritualistic sense, so it can resonate in the higher sphere. By this route, it becomes capable of overcoming the neurosensory bond and of connecting with its own extrahuman source.

We must not forget that the human being conditioned by corporality, as human–animal, cannot be of value except through the dialectics of itself, that is, by means of thought bound to the neurosensory system. It is the human that should be overcome and that is ordinarily overcome only thanks to death. Therefore, the initiation into the New Mysteries is a path of will, which needs thinking suitable to the "beyond-human" dimension, or to the Logos of the Resurrection, to achieve independence from animal–dialectical corporality, during life. It is the corporality in which the animal element is degraded in a way that is not possible for a full-fledged animal.

The paths that assume the Logos have been outdated by ignoring the secret correlation that already exists within the human soul, namely the present possibility of the connection between the "I" and the heart's etheric light—which is to say, with what is described as the secret of the solar sacrarium. Such a connection rigorously involves the liberation of thinking (insofar as it is the conscious thought of the present-day human being), that is to say, it involves the liberation of the soul, there, where it is crucified by the demand of instincts and passions, by being subjected to the cerebral system—a subjection for which nature, pure in itself, is corrupted as human–animal nature.

The undertaking of the Grail is the soul's liberating action within the sphere of the corporeal system, which binds it to earthliness for the production of thinking consciousness. Therefore, thought is the head of the serpent that must be grasped, just like within thinking lies the force that must be recuperated. Any orientation toward the Grail that ignores the spiritual practice of thinking as indicated can indeed prompt the spirit of the research, but not lead it to fulfillment. Obstructors today inspire a path of Manas without Logos, or with an artificial, "paradisiacal" Logos—namely, without the real subject of the experience. The subject cannot discover itself if it does not possess the vehicle by means of which it immediately expresses itself in the world, and if it does not re-ascend the current of thinking—which is such a vehicle—until encountering the cosmic element of consciousness.

11

ANDROGYNY AND ISIS–SOPHIA

The soul is the seat of the contemplation of the New Mysteries, the guardian of the suprasensory processes of consciousness, of the secret life of thought, the unknown bearer of the wisdom of everlasting things. This wisdom is the eternal Sophia, identifiable as the symbolic Virgin Sophia, or the constitutional purity that the soul has lost. It is the Isis Lucifer kidnapped from Osiris and who, consequently, is waiting to be freed from within Lucifer's kingdom.

We must enter that kingdom with forces of total self-giving. To enter there is a precondition for accessing the New Mysteries, or the sacrarium of the Grail. But for such an undertaking, adequate means are necessary—not doctrines, which not only lack power over the Adversary, but are the Adversary's hidden instrument. The same path of thinking risks becoming a path of pride and of sublime egoism if it does not lead to the consecration of itself to the Divine and to the limitless love for one's neighbor—indeed, the discovery of Isis–Sophia.

To realize the pure intellect, or the original mediation of thought, is not yet to discover Isis–Sophia. All meditative techniques today undergo the harm of the constitutional dis-animation of thought. Some of them can, nonetheless, allow the spiritual practitioner to discover the pure movement. The pure movement, as intuition restored to thought, can probe the world's initial extra-dialectical background without awareness of the ideational–imaginative forces set into motion. The human intellectual or dialectical movement, bound to corporality, thus maintains its underlying control. For this reason, knowledge of the perennial essences—the key to the reintegration—remains silent, hermetically imperceptible. Despite spiritual practice, the soul minimally overcomes the condition of captivity and of deafness, precisely in the state of reflectivity. It remains *limited* to a human perception of itself, non-cosmic, non-extrahuman, as it really is.

The intellect that reaffirms itself according to the rediscovered inner movement of thinking, but without discovering the secret of the soul's life, or without liberating Isis–Sophia, continues to undergo the deep unconscious bond. Unknowingly, in being strengthened, it still obeys the power of destitute nature, devoid of Logos.

However, if this intellect moves according to the ancient paths of the spirit, with the wisdom of the past, it cannot realize the relation that the soul had to the world before the fall into reflectivity, or before the age of self-consciousness and of freedom, because it undergoes the harm of reflectivity without being able to know its suprasensory counterpart, or the moment of self-determination as a moment of identity with the Logos. It lacks the illuminating connection with Isis–Sophia. The soul is essentially fortified within the sphere of its own alienation, unknowingly. Though it has the capacity of magical movement, it has at its disposal a life that is not derived from the source of life but, rather, from reinforced reflectivity. The human–animal limit continues to condition it.

The path to the Logos, however, is closed off to the intellect, which, by means of new forms, confines Isis–Sophia to dialectical consciousness. Dialectical consciousness, based unconsciously on feeling rather than on thought, can believe itself to be "traditional." Comforted by philological culture and by symbolic sagacity, it can pursue the persuasion of a restored wisdom of perennial things—a deception not unlike that of materialistic dialecticism. The naïvety of such consciousness is its inability to recognize the thinking arising from the Logos, capable of translating the doctrines of the Tradition in terms of intuition and current logic.

The *dogma* of super-nature is only as good as that of nature. They are the same dogma. They are the valence of a metaphysical alterity opposite the human being as the subject that conceives it and, in conceiving it, is unaware that it begins to overcome it. This conceiving is taken away from the subject; the relation is no longer possible; the subject has before it only the symbol of its own alienation. If such a situation is translated into "doctrine," the subject, in whose depths alone the Logos can surface, is in doctrinaire form unconsciously eliminated.

Today, the Western solar path holds true for every spiritual practitioner on Earth who genuinely seeks the original life of the light. Isis–Sophia is the symbol of this original life that connects the soul with the Divine—the secret weaving of the soul, which the soul can no longer perceive, since it unconsciously lives only in the reflection. It is not the mere mystical force, nor only the transcendent virtue of feeling but, rather, the "feminine" polarity of the soul as the celestial intellect, with respect to the "masculine" polarity of the spirit as will—namely, the soul's original nature, the intuitive virtue of divine things, which in the beginning expressed itself as the power of love. In fact, it constituted the soul's life of the light before its imprisonment within the kingdom of Lucifer, or within the sphere of the alternating psychic sequence of exultation and depression. The life of the light truly is what becomes human love in the incarnate soul.

Feeling that feels as a result of thinking's fall into reflectivity is ruled unopposed by Lucifer, who indeed renders it capable of resonating spiritually—though not beyond the limits of reflected egoity—through the continuous oscillation of attraction and of repulsion, of exultation and of desperation, duality with no way out, the very limit of human love. It is this feeling that invades the soul, by means of mystical or spiritual tensions. With respect to it, however, the investigator knows that, in modern times, the possibility to determine abstract and calculable physical reality temporarily renders reflected thinking independent of the luciferic psyche. A passage toward overcoming the oscillation is opened, but it is not conscious.

Constitutionally, the feminine polarity of the soul expresses itself in mental picturing, while the masculine polarity expresses itself in willing. The element of the will is inserted in the mental picturing turned determinately toward the measurable world. But the marriage of the two polarities is rendered unproductive by the reflected state. The androgynous germ of the soul is isolated; its cosmic power remains silent and ignored. The task of the spiritual practitioner is to re-enliven it, there, where it is devoid of its current of life.

When the will spontaneously flows in mental picturing, we have "imagining." Such imagining, nonetheless, normally expresses the realm of Lucifer, given that his impulse is not pure or conscious willing. The life that he bears comes from feeling. By this route, Isis–Sophia remains prisoner of the reflected psyche, the kingdom of Lucifer. In the "imagining," however, the conscious will can be inserted, which is to say, the "masculine" element of willing can be united with the "feminine" element of mental picturing. In this union, the soul's androgynous germ is reawakened. The liberation of Isis–Sophia from the realm of Lucifer begins through the higher androgynous operation where original love is revived.

Thinking and the will are two polar opposite forces, in continuous combination. Thinking is awake, but devoid of life. The will is immersed in deep sleep, but it is the bearer of life. Thinking, however, can arouse the profound will, as is normally the case when simple "mental picturing" arouses the movement of the limbs. This possibility for thinking to *descend* into the motor will of the limbs, is the point of departure or the secret of the reconnection of the two forces according to an original cosmic power. Such power can be recognized as the current of the "I" independent of the psyche in the soul, that is, independent of Lucifer's influence.

The pure intellect can rise to the point of connecting with the Logos, if it discovers the Virgin Sophia, which is the imagination liberated from the realm of Lucifer. It is the feeling that rises up to the degree that it no longer feels according to Lucifer, or according to reflected egoity, to gather what the feeling of Lucifer always excludes, namely the Logos content of each entity, as well as of each event. Due to the absence of such content, we suffer and rejoice illusorily, because we behave as if that (content) were graspable by the reflected consciousness, continuously carrying out the *unreal* experience of the being that appears *real* to us—never having things, for the fact that we do not have their Essence.

When we speak of living thinking, we are actually alluding to the inner animating force symbolized by the Virgin Sophia. Dialectical thought is what has lost the secret of the Virgin Sophia and imprints feeling with that loss. When the fire of light of the "I" lights up within the astral body through an act of conscious thinking, the light of Lucifer is momentarily redeemed by the light of the Logos. The unconscious germ of the liberation of the Virgin Sophia is enlivened. This germ can become conscious edifying life, if it is perceived as the inner nucleus of the idea.

Feeling that continuously suffers and rejoices through an identical process is the virtue of the Virgin Sophia, the prisoner of Lucifer. Feeling asks that it not be eliminated but, rather, freed from the human–animal level, or from the rational soul. That is to say, it seeks to irradiate its real life. This is the symbolic Sophia, the virtue of living thinking. It alone can feel the Logos according to the primordial musicality, but it cannot do this, if it is not liberated. This liberation comes from the restored marriage between thinking and the will, which, as an initial androgynous experience, is the modern path to renewing the Mysteries, or divine magic. Leading to the initiation of the new times, thinking finds its own volitional source—the synthesis of the soul's masculine and feminine polarity.

Celestial love is the true meaning of human love. All human love unknowingly moves from its celestial content, but without the hope of realizing it, because within the sphere of the psyche it endures the imprisonment of Lucifer, the enchantment of the appearing, which, assumed as reality through reflected consciousness, but with the power of the "I," or with the spirit's force that nevertheless lies behind (the scenes), generates irresistible desire, the continuous greed of the ephemeral and its delusion.

The greatest impediment to the experience of Androgyny, or to the real initiatory path, is the unconscious vampirism of feeling, which continuously alters the emotional life and, therefore, the equilibrium of the soul. For this reason, today there appear magical paths that propose the *most cushy independence* from emotionality, the one that eliminates, within the soul, the element of compassion and of understanding. From this elimination springs an indisputable force, capable of magical heights, which does not, however, come from the "I" but, rather, from its opposite. The danger for the modern esotericist is, in fact, to conquer the cushy force, at the cost of an animic castration, whose symbol in the Grail legend is Klingsor, and whose modern champions were Aleister Crowley and George Gurdjieff.

The transcendent calm, the independence of luciferic feeling, do not come from giving the green light to the "ahrimanic double," that is, to the "being–foundation" of the force of the *ego*, whose undeniable power on the vital–animal level is cynicism and whose possibility of independence from emotions essentially lies in wickedness. This is essentially a vampirism far graver than the emotional luciferic one. True independence from luciferic emotionality comes from a capacity of limitless self-giving, which contains the whole force of emotionality, but it transcends this force because of thinking's connection to the will, in whose current operates the "I," the true victor of the human, because it conquers the two obstructors. It is the one that creatively makes use of their force, according to the spirit. The true correlation of love is born from the spirit capable of being independent from either emotionality, or cushy mysticism, on the one hand, or from egoistic imperturbability, or a cushy magical force, on the other.

The path that reconnects thinking to its metaphysical source opens the passage to love and edifies life and the real relationship of fraternity by overcoming the luciferic vampirism of possessive affection and the ahrimanic vampirism of eliminating feeling, or the false magical force. The soul can be revived thanks only to the original force of the "I." But it needs the secret of the connection with the Logos—above all, the memory of the connection.

Isis–Sophia is the soul's original level that is lost, namely the memory of the spirit, the primordial light of the heart, unseen—the real content of being. This appears to lie beyond thinking, because the original identity of being and thinking is lost. This original identity is precisely the primordial, but forgotten, sound of the androgynous nucleus of the soul. For this reason, the world appears objective, outer, matter of fact, and devoid of Logos, graspable only by means of calculation and dialectics.

Thought's reconnection to the "I" is the initial movement of the magical will, the act of freedom possible only for the self-conscious human being. The pure connectivity of dialectical thinking can lead the investigator to intuit a similar logic of living thinking—namely the autonomy of this (living thinking) with respect to the senses and the psyche, its possibility of bestowing the initial experience of the "subtle body." But this is not yet to discover the Logos. On the contrary, this is the moment in which a spiritual practitioner runs the risk of unconsciously using the acquired virtue of pure thinking

against the Logos, according to a residual impulse of the fundamental egoic nature. Such a spiritual practitioner can become the
instructor of many disciples eager to depend on teachers who show,
dialectically, that they possess the way.

The path of thinking risks becoming a path of sublime egoism, if
the light of Isis–Sophia fails to illuminate it. There is a possible point
of arrest in the sphere of esoteric intellectualism, endowed with its
inner dynamics and even its powers, which are certainly limited. We
can speak about the path's area of arrest, at the level of an esoteric
organic intellectualism, incapable of a radical connection with the
"I," or with the Logos. It is an area that can be overcome only if we
radically pursue the spiritual practice of thinking, so that it opens
the path to the heart—from which, the memory of divine things,
Isis–Sophia, is resurrected.

To overcome the neutral zone, where sentient cowardice or the
intellect's betrayal is continuously able to return, there must be a
transference from the soul's subsistent way of being to an original,
but lost way of being, which was necessary to lose to get it back
from a level of spontaneity to one of freedom—namely, the memory
of the perennial essences, which is the internal structure of the soul
that is lost—eliminated by dialectical–sensual consciousness.

The soul's original state of being is resurrected to the extent
that it manages to contemplate, *outside* of itself, what has become
an inner process to it, namely the forming of the idea, creative
imagining. This imagining is *feeling* that has been freed, which
turns toward the area where the power of the reawakened ancient
faith, the virtue of absolute self-consecration, can light up, like a
flame of divine love. It is prepared by the marriage of thought and
the will.

Thinking arouses the motor will in the limbs. Each time a thought
or an image is translated into a movement of the limbs, the magical

will lights up in the astral body and permeates the etheric all the way to the physical. The technique of the magical will consists in realizing movements that incarnate specific mental commands and in imaginatively perceiving the golden light of the will within those movements. It is to contemplate the ongoing current of the will and, simultaneously, to experience its absolute autonomy with respect to the psyche or to the astral body. This autonomy is perceived as the higher power of the "I," its Olympian impersonality. It is important for the disciple to perceive the purity of this will current as a luminous life of the soul, independent of the greedy psyche and, therefore, essential as a *measure* of the purity of the current of *eros*, which it is before being the sensual animal current.

A development of such a technique consists in imagining the movement of the limbs, even while one is immobile. One imagines and contemplates a position of the limbs that differs from that in which one effectively finds oneself. Then one achieves this position and imagines the actual one that preceded it. Furthermore, by remaining in an immobile state, one can imagine a continuous movement of the limbs (e.g., walking or running), thereby perceiving the autonomy of the current of willing.

These exercises of imagination–contemplation reawaken the thinking within the current of the will and the will within the current of thinking. The inner force that they awaken does not know any other limit than the soul's incapacity to gather it in its fullness. But it is the same marriage of thinking and the will that prepares the soul to overcome the instinctive egoic opposition to the flowing of the powerful impersonality of the force.

The will must be willed so that the metaphysical force can incarnate, but it does not have any other arouser and operator than thinking. The will actually moves from thinking, but thinking really moves from the will because, in real metaphysics, will and thinking constitute a single force. The secret of the whole spiritual practice is the human realization of this force.

It is not enough to discover pure thinking, pure perceiving. The spiritual practice of perceiving and of thinking realizes an initial and momentary independence from the realm of the psyche, symbolically from the kingdom of Lucifer. True independence is what is realized with respect to the kingdom of Ahriman, the donor of the *cushy force*, since it is the real enslaver of the "I."

The soul's contradiction is being bound to corporality and, nonetheless, yearning for its own liberation by means of the consciousness founded on such a bond. On the other hand, the independence attributable to spiritual practice is momentary; the light it produces becomes the spiritual nutriment of the psyche hungry for appearance and sensual expression if the connection with Isis–Sophia does not manifest. The inner individuality, reinforced but not freed, can become even more subtly fond of life, as sensory *maya*.

There is an impulse, without which one does not proceed— namely, an impulse that cannot come from magical sensational representations, but only from the capacity to comprehend earthly error and to be compassionate toward fellow human beings. It is a sentiment of love, which springs as an authentic force of the "I," from thinking's profound agreement with the will. It is the love born from the impulse of the inconceivable, superconscious absolute—the memory of the original quality that alone can remind the soul of its true nature, or reawaking from the Lethean sleep of aversion overcoming the prosaic relation with the world devoid of Logos.

Once Isis–Sophia is found, the Logos is found. The Logos virginally fertilizes the soul. This moment coincides with the apparition of the solar sacrarium. The presence of the Logos is realized because it is perceived. Even if present, it cannot be realized if it goes unperceived. The organ of perception is the volitional power of thinking, or the current in which thinking is one with the will.

The "arid," yet luminous, path of thinking leads to the discovery of Isis–Sophia, because it is the path that is absolutely a-psychic. The secret musicality of the soul is discovered as a structural

force, beyond that realm of the prosaic, the realism of the calculable or the nonexistent. The poetic state is not the calling of
the unreal but, rather, the secret logic of the soul, the relation
supernally mathematical, because it is rhythmical all the way to
the "harmony of spheres." The *lost logic* of the soul is truly what
is called Virgin Sophia.

This logic can be rediscovered, because in germ it emerges in
intuitive thinking. The spiritual practice of thinking leads to the
articulation in images of the original thinking, images that make its
transcendent content visible. The immediate life of such thought is
precisely creative imagining.

Ordinary imaging is subject to reflected consciousness. Therefore, irrespective of its "expanding," it does not escape the
luciferic prison of the psyche. Intuitive imagining overcomes the
psychic limit and frees the soul from the realm of Lucifer. It is the
liberation of celestial feeling, which overcomes aversion and realizes compassion. The investigator begins to find the knowledge of
divine things, or the Virgin Sophia, giving life through imaginative forms to the soul's androgynous principle—the marriage of
"mental picturing" and willing. This marriage begins when feeling
participates not only as a latent force of consecration, but even as
a conscious movement toward the synthesis of thinking and willing, which can be actualized by means of the correct concentration, the correct meditation.

Such participation is the lighting up of feeling by virtue of the
ultimate purpose by which we, as investigators, experience the
spiritual practice of thinking—namely, the profound intent we
introduce into the act of concentration–meditation. The purity of
this intent is the measure of the act's spiritual potential in which
lies the lamp of the thinking will. The limit of Lucifer, overcome
within the intent, is therefore not overcome within the soul. However, the synthesis of thinking and willing can give such intent an
operating power. It can take it to meet the impersonal virtue that

corresponds to it—the light's original virtue. The encounter with the Virgin of the light is essentially the encounter with the light of the Logos, which cannot occur if it were not for the androgynous synthesis of forces.

12

The Secret of Meditation

We have indicated a path of thinking, inasmuch as it alone leads to the perception of the cosmic process that takes place behind the scenes of consciousness, whenever the "I" encounters the human astral, through the thinking act. This higher moment of thinking must be known by a conscious spiritual practitioner. Thought, rationality, and the reasoning of both philosophers and psychologists is not real thinking but, rather, its lower manifestation. Even when a pure intuition acquires the form of thinking, the thinker does not experience such intuition but, rather, its dialectical guise.

The suprasensory experience consists in discovering, through the strengthening of the will, the *cosmic connection* of thought, by exhausting its dialectical form. Naturally, the inner light, present within each thought, disappears in the dialectical process, so as to be urgently needed in the form of the thought immediately following. This inner light gives initial life to dialectics, which, simultaneously eliminates it to be formally recognizable, to be human thought. The human being's true force appears in the moment that precedes—not temporarily—conscious thought. However, this conscious thought is the only activity of consciousness capable of finding the true force within itself, as its own self-transcendence.

As human beings, we are each continuously at the limit of our own power, or of our own perennial being. We continuously presuppose an unalterable current of life, which does not incarnate, which does not flow in us, because we close ourselves off to it. We reject it, because we need thought that takes on our animal needs, which rise to a psychic and even spiritual necessity. Today, there are spiritual systems, which, despite their aristocratic guise, essentially do not overcome that level. They would not know how to indicate a path toward the perception of the cosmic power of the light that pre-dialectically burns at each rising of thought, like a fire of the consciousness soul, to which dialectics, as a form of fear, is normally opposed, the awareness of it slipping away. They would not know how to indicate it, because, despite the metaphysical object, their inner level is that of dialectics, where the spirit is opposed. We can say that such paths have the function of obstructing the real suprasensory experience of today's human being and of supplying the factory of spiritual misfits who will talk their whole life about spirit, about initiation and about esotericism, without knowing where these reside.

Just as materialists picture nature that, outside them, came to be on its own, esotericists picture a tradition that exists through its own power and allows itself to be known by them—esotericists who, to find it, need only to make philological and mystical contact with the form it assumed at a given point in time and in a specific place. Esotericists who do not recognize the typical spiritual practice of thinking presently demanded by the consciousness soul lack the ability to distinguish the soul's element of perpetuity from the formal dialectical element.

What the human is according to the dialectical consciousness that expresses it, is not the genuine human, but the human–animal that we must overcome. Our presence on Earth has this purpose. The constant exploding of evil, as well as the ongoing limit of death, are, for us, a sign of the non-awareness, or ignorance, of such a purpose.

The human is that in which desire is totally interwoven. Normally, we need death so that we can be freed of it. On the other hand, volitional disentanglement during life is the real elaboration of the human, the relation with the Essence, which we must realize insofar as we are alive and conscious, not because of death.

If the detachment and the contemplation conferred by death can be realized by ascetic virtue, as an impetus of life, during life, investigators essentially confront consciously the powers of a death continuously followed by the Resurrection. The investigator discovers that life, itself untouched by death, is what is imperceptible and sustains animal existence. But, there, where it is not engaged in this vital process, it surfaces without allowing itself to be perceived as thought, which bears within itself the original cosmic impulse.

Without allowing itself to be perceived; this is what we, as investigators of the new times, must understand. If we come to perceive the moment in which the "I" encounters the astral to generate thought, we encounter a cosmic process. To perceive the life that continuously annihilates itself as dialectical thought is the secret to the reintegration of thinking and of the human being—the possibility of experiencing the living element of nature and history, the initial solution to human problems, the true sense of the manifesting of thought.

Thought is not a human production, but something that gives itself to us and with which we are wrong to identify. It continuously gives itself to us as a *symbol* of the original life that is lost. Apart from being a symbol, thought is *maya*. To perceive thinking is to perceive life, namely the flaming creative light, the magical force. Thought is the suprasensory world that manifests to us just as the sensory world manifests to us on the physical plane.

Imperceptible life leaves its mark directly on the pre-dialectical element that is immediate to thinking and that permeates perception. Dialectical thought is the *maya* of pre-dialectical thinking, just like perception is the *maya* of the suprasensory manifesting, for which perception *appears* complete in itself, without the pre-dialectical element that continuously operates in it.

The element of life, as an element of perpetuity, and therefore immortality, is the timeless antecedent of thought, the suprasensory immediacy of thought, not that of feeling or the will, which move in their element of life, as has been shown, thanks to the inner mediation of thinking, under the sign of spontaneity. Content of thinking always solicits emotionality and impulsivity.

Human thought, as dialectical thought, cannot think the Logos. It can only operate on itself to gather its life. Dialectical thought cannot grasp the Logos, just as the hand aimed high cannot grasp the sky. The deception of dialectical thought is not to know its own limit, which, as has been seen, is the reflected state. Thus, it can discursively philosophize on all that is suprasensory, ignoring that the suprasensory is such because it lies beyond such a limit. It is the limit that dialectical thinking undergoes unknowingly and, yet, it is the only unknown that it can come to know and, therefore, possess through its very own transcendence.

Human thought cannot think the Logos, but it can find itself within the Logos. There, where the "I" encounters the astral body, thought arises as the *flaming light*, endowed with creative power because it rises up from the Logos. This light of fire is continuously extinguished in dialectical consciousness. The deception of the dialectical movement is that it turns toward everything, but it cannot conceive turning toward itself. It conceives everything, but not the path that leads it to perceive its own life of light. It is the path that it already follows to be reflected, or dialectical—the only one, however, unknown to thinking.

In being reflected, human thought opposes the Logos, but, there, where it is not yet reflected and it has its intuitive moment, it moves as the fire of light of the Logos. The Logos itself enables reflectivity, in whose opposition to the Logos we, as humans, realize freedom. But it is the freedom that must enable each of us to find, as a free being, the Logos from which we move.

The secret of healing the human being lies in perceiving the light of fire, of which thought pre-dialectically burns. The illness we endure originates from the loss of the flaming light of the Logos. The illness of the soul, the illness of the body, the illness of feeling and willing, is actually the illness of thinking obscured and devoid of the power of life, endowed with the power of death. Human illness begins within thought. Within thought lies the possibility of healing. We must, however, enter into the secret of thinking. We must realize that it is not a rational path, but a path of the will. The will overcomes rationality, but it must first possess the process of this rationality to be able to transcend it; to overcome the process by means of which death continuously eliminates life within thinking.

The Logos always manifests as a flash of (the) "light of fire," from the "burning bush" to the dazzling light of Paul on the road to Damascus. From the moment the Logos incarnated and defeated death, we have had the possibility to think according to the Resurrection, insofar as the flaming light of the Logos lights up within each thought that we think. But to perceive this light, we must overcome the *darkness* of dialectical thought. Only such perception reconnects the soul to the dazzling original light of the Logos.

✶

The element of perpetuity is the universal continuum of thinking, which can take on error or the psychic content, by contradicting its own nature and becoming the thinking of the particular on the plane of reflectivity. The error of thought is not to know that it continuously connects the *particular* with the universal, that is, not to truly be thinking, because the particular as such really *does not exist* for thought, which in itself is whole. This is not a philosophical issue but, rather, one of practical spiritual practice and redemption, according to the petition of reflected dialectics, for which reflection continuously contradicts the light. The particular does not exist outside the universal, except for fallen thought, incapable of realizing, through thinking, its own power of life, which is the life of the light.

The suprasensory is not the suprasensory that is thought, or felt, or intuited, but the suprasensory *within* thinking, the "within itself" of thinking, its movement of life—the movement of life that thought continuously demands for dialectification, which, in fact, continuously extinguishes such movement. It continuously demands this movement so as to extinguish it.

This extinction is necessary for dialectical thought, for its own expression on the sensory plane. In reality, it takes place to open the passage to the free inner act, which we, however, are unable to carry out. The extinction should have its own compensation in a restitution of the element of life by the thinking that, through rigorous self-awareness, completes the process, grasping its own movement and its current of life, or the power of consciousness, to which at last the sensory world directly reveals its content. This is the spiritual practice of the new times, the most opposed and the least understood, even by those who presume to be its custodians.

The question of freedom is precisely this: It is the use of the extinction of the original living element, or the use of the *void* produced by the extinction. If it does not become the path of a ready and energetic will, ascetically prepared, that void is filled by the vital element of psychophysiological nature. Ordinarily, we feel compensated for the death of the original element of the life of thought, by something that is more than thought, because it has within it a force, but of a vital–animal nature. Therefore, we cannot believe that from thought the spirit can come as a force. We thus choose a path of freedom unconsciously bound to physical nature.

Under these circumstances, if we turn toward the spiritual, we avoid the path of thinking, which appears to us devoid of inner life, and we follow a path of feeling and of will that cannot lead us beyond the limits of the sentient soul, or of the human–animal, because it does not leave the neurosensory system. Within our own limited subjectivity, we elaborate a yogic or mystical or mediumistic path, by means of which the vacuum of the spirit is filled with spiritualistic emotionalism, with sacralized sensuality, or with rhetorical ethics.

We shun our own liberation by way of materialistic and spiritualistic paths. We nullify the inner subject by projecting opposite us a total physical reality, as well as a total metaphysical reality. We want to depend on reality, not knowledge. But it is a reality imagined, not possessed. In that projection, there is everything, except the human subject.

The deception of everyday life arises from the degraded universality of thought that, at each level of its degradation, becomes a form of the knowledge that corresponds to it. But, at each level, thought is also the vehicle of discovery of our own universal power in relation to the contingency of the content.

The error is never the real error but, rather, the error of thinking. But not even the error of thinking can be put forward as an error, since thought, any thought, in itself, is a force. The error is not to possess this force, but to be possessed by it. The error is the universal that does not know itself with respect to the moment in which, on the reflected plane, it becomes the form of a particular content. Sentient subjective nature uses thought as a typical vestment. This thought is the universal, but as reflection it lacks the power of the universal. The reflected form, opposite the universal, thus becomes the vestment of the error, which appears as reality and has the power to move the life of the soul until influencing the rhythm of the blood, and that of the nerves, to the point of corrupting life.

Such a process, however, is reversible. The reflection can mediate its own light *if the "I" is active within it*. The "I" can operate by means of the reflection or by means of determined thought, which bears within itself, as we have seen, the power of *a-psychicness* and impersonality. The right technique of concentration realizes such a possibility. The universal in thought can connect its own substance with the power of the form, so that the particular, the error, the psychic content, can dissolve and the forces engaged in them converge again toward their center of life.

The magic of thinking, which we unknowingly use daily, against the wellbeing of the soul and the body, can be realized in accordance with its pre-dialectical creative direction. It is not a matter of changing thought but, rather, of willing it, of intensifying it, as it is. Thought, fortified, is enlivened of its own inner power, which is the power of the Logos. Lifeless and reflected, it is the vehicle of the powers adverse to the Logos. *Erroneous thought does not exist*; only reflected thought exists. Any thought, by losing reflectivity to the degree that it is strengthened, becomes the vehicle for the power of the Logos, the power of the invincibility of the "I." The destructive process of thinking is reversible, thanks to the volitional act that grasps the reflected determination and makes it its own by drawing from the original moment of the process. With the magic of thinking, we can change our own destiny and the destiny of others, not by means of will, but according to suprasensory guidance.

By liberating thought, we can know the series of dependencies of our inner life and resolve them. The inner life has only one center, the higher "I," or Logos, which is avoided through a dependence on the values of reflected vision. The series of dependencies is the series of fictitious human values. Such values are symbols of the contents' alteration, which cannot be overcome simply because they are perceived as illusory. The magic of thinking must bring about their conversion, the continuous transformation of error into truth.

The world's evil can be avoided through spiritual wisdom, but it cannot be resolved in this way. Spiritual wisdom is the subtlest form of evil, perpetuated through various forms of spiritualism devoid of the Logos. Inner development leads spiritual practitioners to glimpse the secret connections of evil within human nature in religious, ethical, theological, and ideological forms. Evil is the illegitimate use of the universal in thinking, an illegitimate use that is possible given that reflected thought is grasped by our instinctive nature, which takes the place of the "I."

It is inevitable that, by moving from the thinking–Logos, the spiritual practitioner encounters the evil of human nature. This encounter takes place within the depths of consciousness and is the heroic operation of transformation, or of conversion, of the erroneous content. The soul overcomes an ulterior zone of non–self-awareness and, therefore, of dependence on the darkness, from which pain, desire, anguish, hate, and so on, continuously arise. They ascend, justified by reason and by facts, according to an incontrovertible legitimacy, but precisely by means of this, they destroy the structures of the soul and of the body. They devour life.

We must objectively place the psychic content before us and penetrate it with thinking. We must integrate it with the thinking that it lacks—namely, with the current of will from which it normally escapes. It is anguish or desire or fear because it has inverted the relationship. It maneuvers thought. The exercise of concentration and of the objectification of thought enables us to penetrate the erroneous content with volitional power. At first, conscious attention turns to its real meaning. It translates it into the content of an idea, or into integral thinking. The operation leads to the possibility of willing the internal substance of the erroneous psychic content, which is disintegrated by this willing.

There is no psychic movement, which, however obscure and impulsive, cannot be converted into its exact content of thought. This content can be willed from within, or permeated by the thinking will, which transforms its substance by rediscovering its pure force. In reality, each impulsive current is moved by a thought that escapes consciousness, insofar as it is controlled by sentient feeling and willing, or by that current of the animic body that we, as humans, have in common with the animal. One can say that each psychic movement moves by means of a germinal thought led to act in a way opposite that of the thinking of autonomous consciousness.

Our art is to arrive at identifying the inverse germination of thinking, until perceiving it. At first, we carry out an analysis that moves by virtue of the thinking force, rather than by virtue of dialectics. The identification of the instinctive movement's germinal thinking must become so concrete as to become perception. In that way, it rises as an image in movement—an image in search of its own altered reality. Its movement is redeemed, allowing itself to be permeated by the willed imaging with which we meet it. This imagining is prepared in meditation.

As investigators, we must initially envision to ourselves, as objectively as possible, the instinctive situation that we go through, until translating it into the pure power of thought. We realize, in its presence, the same autonomy that we grasped through the spiritual practice of perceiving, by training ourselves to have the pure content of a sensory object. However, we cannot initially have the instinctive content in the pure state, except as a concept. By means of contemplative persistence, this concept is translated into a volitional process, in which the current of will releases and transforms the psychic content. The process manifests as an image. The contemplation of the image coincides with the content's transformation into a spiritual content, which is perceived as the initial current of life that flows in place of the instinctive current. With practice, the image can be possessed to such an extent that it can be continuously set against the sudden rising of an irregular impulse.

The living current of thinking bears the transformative force of the Logos into the sphere of instincts. The investigator can attain the capacity of a direct action of the will in such a sphere.

❦

The direct magic of thinking is "its grasping" the direction of the Logos within itself, the elevating of itself to its own pre-dialectical moment. It is normally incapable of such elevation unless it moves from a dialectical structure. In fact, we have seen how it is possible within the vehicle of a dialectical sequence, to insert the "I" into the pure connection, by overcoming formal discursive conscious-ness and the sensory correlation, until experiencing the very force of the connection, which touches the center of the heart.

This conjunction can be realized at its very inception. But it is naïve to attempt it prior to the lucid possession of the pre-dialectical sequence. Previously, it was to reconnect thought to its source of life. Now, it is to experience the point at which thought, through its rebirth, encounters such a source.

Notwithstanding the fact that it is reborn pure insofar as it is pre-dialectical, thought nevertheless undergoes duality. As human thought, it is not pure spiritual life. Now, it can be born one with the Logos, realizing, beyond the death of dialectics, the human–divine synthesis, which prepares for the restitution of the "primor-dial state," namely the resurrection from the death of dialectics. It proceeds by opening up to its own movement, which it already knows as a non-dialectical movement. Each moment of this opening up to itself is soon followed by the precise moment of awareness of the continuity.

The continuity ceases to be supported by punctuality. It becomes pure instantaneousness, when non-dialectical thought is *struck* by the Logos. Thought rises again, fleetingly, as the lightning bolt of the Logos.

This experience, which can be realized to the extent that divine will responds to the maximum of individual will, enables the spiritual practitioner to contemplate, inwardly, the images of the path completed by the "I" in earthly evolution, namely the "images-force" given by the Master of the New Times to arouse, contemplatively, the itinerary toward the restoration of the Primordial State, insofar as the "I"–Logos is perceived within the consciousness soul.

We have been able to show how such a possibility presupposes the resurrection of thought from the state of death implicit to its separation from its own original nucleus of life. What is split, reflected, abstract, and lifeless to the extent that it is dialectical, reconnects with its own original virtue, reconstituting a unity, which, if it is nourished by its own "images-force," is translated into vision. This vision, howsoever accorded by the spiritual world, is necessary, since it frees the etheric "imagining" from the anthropomorphic impression. It is an event–model that *in a germinal way* realizes, within the soul, the reintegration of the human being, to which the Logos has opened the door through incarnation, death and Resurrection.

This cosmic impulse of thinking is one with super-individual feeling and willing. It does not belong to individual nature, in spite of being the power that elevates it. Descending into the current of instincts, it directly brings about its transformation, by initially separating the pure force from that to which it is longingly bound. The impurity is always animal nature embroiled in sensation, whose objective content it does not control, for it is controlled by it. The cosmic impulse of thinking bears the eliminating power of each and every adherence of the psyche to nature. It has within it the timeless virtue of the rhythm, necessary to the insistence on instantaneousness, by means of which the Divine connects with the human. In instantaneousness, the Logos appears as the lightning bolt. This lightning bolt transforms instinct. Simultaneously, it extinguishes it and re-emanates it as the power of the spirit.

Persistence in concentration has as its aim the achievement of this resplendent moment, without which the human's animal element cannot be resolved. The human being, as a human–animal, must be overcome, otherwise it subtly controls the whole work, always reducing it to its own secret bondage. The animal limit that has to be overcome continuously arises in concentration.

Resplendent thought has the power of the profound circulation and of the resolution of what in human evil has the power of radicalness, which cannot be reached except by the lightning-bolt Logos of thinking, whose force on Earth arises from fulfilling the divine task at the roots of the human being—namely, the victory over death, the Resurrection.

The real function of thinking is to become the vehicle of the Resurrection. We have been able to show how thought is only a symbol of its own force. In fact, as rational thought it rises from the extinction of this force. However, for this reason the very extinction of thought becomes the resurrection of the force. Actually, dialectical thought is dead thought, used in error as living thinking. The lightning-bolt Logos of thinking is kindled from the death of dialectical thought, in positive concentration.

Thought demands to be thought until it is no longer a specter of its true being. Thought's true being can be experienced as one with the uncorrupted feeling of the soul. From the resurrection of thought, the purity of feeling is restored; creative faith is resurrected. Isis–Sophia, the Virgin of the light, is reintegrated as the burning life of the soul, without which the initiatory Work is not possible for the human being of the present day.

Therefore, the true being of thought is the Logos of the Resurrection. Until such a true being rises, dialectical thought expresses the anthropomorphic, or human–animal dimension, and it erupts in structures devoid of life. It expresses itself in mechanical structures, whose mighty ingenuity is undoubtedly the work of the spirit. But it ignores the spirit.

To go to the Moon without having fathomed the mystery of the birth of a blade of grass or the inner structure of matter on Earth is to move not in cosmic space (where it is impossible to penetrate by means of machines) but in the space of non-consciousness—namely, to extend non-consciousness by increasing its domain. It means believing that one arrives on the Moon, whereas it is to move from one point of the narrow dual vision of matter to another. Duality is an earthly illness that must be overcome on Earth. It makes no sense to project it into the universe and then believe that we investigate it objectively. *We have never truly reached the Moon*, but only the realm of the image that we make of it according to earthly limits—a photographic image, enlarged, an image by means of which we are at the mercy of animal nature on Earth.

The sad monotony of materialistic investigation is extended to the whole Cosmos, and we fail to notice that we do not escape that cerebral limit, which can only be overcome on Earth through the realization of the true nature of thinking. In fact, we actually penetrate the real Cosmos only after death, when we are no longer prisoners of physical corporality. Thus, the real experience of the spirit begins as a disentanglement of thought from cerebralism. It is a disentanglement by means of which we, in life, cease to be spiritual prisoners of physiological materiality.

※

This disentanglement is an act of freedom whose principle we potentially possess in the opposition of reflected (or dialectical) thought to the original light. The opposition is the state of thought grasped by obstructive forces, thanks to that inertia which remains with us as a legacy of the ancient dependence on revelation. The inertia remains within thinking that does not know how to move freely, because it does not know how to turn to its own source, from which it can seek the whole initiative, the entire decision and all the courage. It is a magical and inexhaustible source that does not function if we do not draw on it. We can tap into it for love to *free our neighbor* from the accusation of an evil that we must overcome within ourselves if we truly want to remove the obstruction from the flow of the Divine in the world.

Free human beings remain prisoners of the corporeal limit, led to a human–animal use of freedom. Human beings renounce experiencing freedom as a dimension independent of corporality or cerebralism, ignoring the act of "thinking free of the senses." The human psyche is enslaved by means of thinking bound to cerebralism, to physical nature, to *eros*, to instincts, to passions, to cerebrations, and so on.

Thinking bound to cerebralism has renounced the ancient metaphysical connection, attaining its own initial autonomy by manifesting through the sensory. It began drawing directly on the spiritual with the initial autonomy. Actually, the spiritual has helped itself to cerebral mediation to arrive at the mathematical–physical connection with the sensory. The initial movement of autonomy, however, was arrested at the stage of cerebral mediation. Regarding the achieved science of the Sensory, thought has not known how to identify with the movement of autonomy that the cognitive process of science has allowed it; rather, it has identified with the cerebral mechanics of the autonomy. It has relied on dialectical freedom, reiterating, with respect to the sensory, the tendency to depend on past suprasensory revelation. Therefore, revelation demands the action of the pure individual element—the decision of direct contact within the soul with the source of the initiative and of the courage. It is a decision for the sake of the human community, since the

Logos, through the individual act, surfaces in the world and tears the human away from animal nature.

From the agnostic point of view, as well as the gnostic, the tendency for thinking to depend on revelation is due to its lack of awareness of its own movement of light and, thus, of the moment of independence that has permitted it to break with the ancient Revelation. The unconscious attitude of dependence is occultly nourished by the demon of matter or of reflected rationality, and by the demon of feeling, for which the control of the soul today is possible to the extent that it is unaware of the new force by means of which it finds itself before matter and before the spirit—namely, the *idea,* which is not the *objectum mentis* of philosophy nor of idealistic dialectics, but rather the presence of the light within thinking of the "I"— namely the power of identity of the "I" with sensory reality, which when freed leads to suprasensory reality, or the foundation.

The dynamic determination of the "I" within the soul by means of the idea, appeals to a new science of meditation. This cannot be the meditation of thinking that used to see the Logos outside of itself, but rather that of thinking that draws on the light of life of the Logos within itself, thereby ceasing to be dialectical.

Thinking that still sees the Logos outside itself is identical to what today sees and thus deifies matter outside itself. In such conditions, contradicting the Logos cannot be avoided. It is inevitable to accuse others, to detest them because of their malice, albeit obvious, whereas the light of the Logos allows each of us to see this same malice arise within our own souls as resentment, accusation, and condemnation pursuant to its further development. It is malice that asks instead to be defeated by the person who is more conscious and stronger thanks to the courage of a free act within the depths of the soul, where the Logos begins to shine.

To discover the Logos within the soul is to free it of accusations toward those who are wrong or otherwise awaken resentment. One becomes grateful toward them, because they help one discover what needs to be overcome within the soul before the Logos can rule there with its pure light. Nor can gratitude be separated from compassion toward them, given that they carry a burden with respect to which they still lack the forces of tolerance and of liberation. It is clear that such understanding toward others according to the Logos is required of all who turn toward the genuine suprasensory, since this understanding is thinking's measure of liberation from the dialectical or human–animal bond, which is the whole point of the spiritual practice of thinking. It is also clear that such an understanding does not exclude the correction of the error, the necessary provisions for eliminating it.

In truth, the purpose of the Logos on Earth is not only to lead humanity back to the Divine—which is the ideal of the Old Testament—but, above all, also to overcome nature within the human being, the nature that continuously corrupts the Divine and corrupts the astral–etheric–physical structure bestowed upon the human being by the Divine. Nature is truly pure, even as fallen nature. It becomes impure within the human being. The fact that animal nature becomes an intelligent power within the human being is the true evil—one that can be overcome only by the force that, in earthly incarnation, tears the human being away from the perishable animal nature. This is the animal nature that penetrates us and even recommends ethical and spiritual means to us. The experience of such a force is for us the real relationship with the Christ.

To rediscover the Logos is the purpose of our present-day crisis and the ultimate meaning of our lives. Our lack of connection with the Logos deprives us of knowing what can unite beings beyond every dissension. It deprives us, in every field, of a real sense of the experience. Numerical and logical rationality lack the power of truth. By leaning exclusively on this (rationality), we cannot but make mistakes in every field. Nevertheless, rationality itself signals the presence of the Logos. The error is not to grasp the Logos where it becomes an activity of consciousness and to seek it by means of soul impulses that essentially reject it, since they reduce it to a cliché necessary to reflected egoity, its ethics, its earthly power, and its dialectics. The Logos of which one speaks politically is not *the* Logos, but its opposite.

To rediscover the Logos is the courageous undertaking of thinking, the courage to find the non-dialectical life of thinking and, therefore, to renew life, thanks to the light from which it springs. It is the courage for the love of truth, which is the love for humanity, the true love, not what expresses itself according to political reason, or out of respect for the myths of the times.

The courage of thinking is not to be subjected to such myths. It is easy to preach peace, love, and justice and to thus give each faction the bait for the accusation of another person's lack of such ideals. The courage of thinking is the courage to overcome dialectics—an overcoming that cannot manifest without the flow of life, thanks to which arises thought. Such life is the Logos. It exists in thought, but this is its *semblance*, even when it is the thought of the spiritual, or the thought of meditation. Needed are spiritual practitioners who discover the *reality* behind the semblance. But such spiritual practitioners must move within the semblance, possess the semblance, if they wish to find what lies beyond it.

To move within the semblance is to move from sensory thought to overcome it. The overcoming is the initial restitution of its inner content. Thus, the Event of Christ is given in a human story, in sensory history, to which we must restore the real, suprasensory content. Nativity, life, communion with the world and with the Disciples, the Passion, death, and the Resurrection, take place as sensory events, in which we must discover the immediate suprasensory content. But this, in turn, refers to the cosmic content. This is the true content, not graspable by dialectical thought, but only by the thinking that overcomes sensory *maya,* which nevertheless overcomes dialectics, both idealistic and materialistic.

True thinking lies beyond the *maya* of what is normally realized as thought, to which the sensory gives form. The sensory world clothes itself with this thought and we look at the world, as if it were that way on its own. We do not recognize there, the vestment of thought, nor the etheric movement by means of which it appears to us. In reality, we think based on such appearing, continuously ignoring the true life of thinking. It is like someone who knows water only with respect to drinking and to the extinction of thirst, knowing nothing of what it is objectively. Likewise, we know thought only as a form of the sensory, or as an abstraction of such a form. We do not know it as the *power* of life in itself—the true "in itself" that we are given to experience and in which, by virtue of identity, we are given to perceive the "in itself" of things.

Healing the human being and, therefore, healing the world begins within this power, because it is the germ of the Logos that has incarnated and defeated death with the Resurrection. Its manifesting results from the death of dialectical thought and the Resurrection of its perennial element, at the level of waking consciousness, where normally perpetuity enters the kingdom of death, which is transitory human "existing." Dialectical thought is a thought already dead; yet, its death bears the germ of the Resurrection. Perpetuity is reborn in the idea, if the idea is conscious of itself.

For the disciple, it is crucial to become aware of the death of dialectical thought. The true sense of concentration and of meditation is the passage from the state of death of dialectical thought to the thinking in which flows the life of the Logos, which has defeated death, because it has defeated the animal nature that possesses life within the human being.

The means by which we think within thought is not discourse or dialectics, and yet it has the power of the logical structure. It is true thinking. This power is to be grasped. As investigators, we discover that from the nothing of dialectics, from the negation of dialectics, from zero, or from the void of dialectics, springs the thinking-force. We need, however, to go beyond to encounter the original power. The Christ is present in this original power, which is the power of dialectical non-thinking, of the non-mental, to which we need to open the passage as we take possession of dialectical thought and control the mental sphere. Without possessing thought or the mental sphere, the lower powers use any silence or void (of the mental sphere) to penetrate the consciousness temporarily bereft of its ordinary defense and to provide the mythical extrasensory experience.

Sensory experience strengthens thinking, because it leads it from the undetermined to the determination, thanks to which the cosmic power of the undetermined indeed limits itself; yet it penetrates the human. Only from the highest forces of the spirit is it possible to descend into the sphere of the senses. The experience of such forces must pass over to conscious spiritual practice, at least initially by a few (individuals), so that the "I" can be awakened within the soul of the world, or within the soul of the community, according to a univocal action within the individual multiplicity.

Thinking is strengthened by means of the determination, but it must use such a force to overcome the limit of the determination, which is dialectics, the mental (activity). It must discover, as living thinking, the power of the undetermined in which flows the real content of the human being—namely, the content of reintegration. Thinking that is arrested at the determination and does not know the force from which it springs, renounces its own element of life, drawing life from the animal support and corrupting such life, while, dialectically, it nourishes itself from the lifeless experience of earthliness, whose symbol is the machine. Such thinking bears with it the inevitability of illness and of death. It deprives us of the original current of life, which is the current of immortality.

Thinking must cognize its own death to restore immortality to the human being. Self-awareness and will have the function of giving the force of its annihilation to thinking, where the lightning flash of the Resurrection is dynamically inherent. This flash is thinking's identity with the Logos, from which the power of the undetermined originates within the determination. For this reason, it is the flash of lightning that shines and resolves the materiality of the Earth.

ABOUT THE AUTHOR

Massimo Scaligero (1906–1980)—born
Antonio Massimo Scabelloni, at Veroli,
in the Frosinone area south of Rome—
received a humanist education, to which
he added the study of logic, mathematics,
and philosophy.

A journalist, poet, writer, scholar, and
deep connoisseur of the esoteric and Eastern philosophy, until 1978
he edited the magazine *East and West*. It was a scientific publica-
tion, in English, to which the leading experts on art, archeology,
philosophy, and religions contributed.

As a young man, Massimo Scaligero had especially intense
spiritual experiences and, for decades, tried to understand their
meaning and nature—until, following the war, he encountered the
thinking of Rudolf Steiner and Anthroposophy. He read Steiner's
Outline of Esoteric Science and found there what his soul had
experienced spontaneously. Thus he recognized the spiritual sig-
nificance of Steiner. He continued his work in Italy following the
death of his master, Giovanni Colazza, who had been a direct pupil
of Rudolf Steiner.

A tireless author and lecturer, he gave two lectures each week
in Rome and dedicated his whole existence to all who sought a
spiritual path during the 1960s and '70s, until his death in Janu-
ary 1980.

Rudolf Steiner set out the basis of his path in *The Philosophy of
Freedom,* and Massimo Scaligero continued the master's work and
its primary instrument, *thinking,* which must become the means of
objective knowledge, a vehicle for transforming the human being
as a whole.

There was superhuman consistency in his life, which included
the marvelous poetry of the pure rhythms of Living Thought.